Digital SAT
Grammar & Punctuation

By

K. Jonathan

Copyright Notice

All rights reserved. Do not duplicate or redistribute in any form.

Introduction

Welcome to Digital SAT - Grammar and Punctuation, a comprehensive resource designed to sharpen your grammar and punctuation skills in preparation for the Digital SAT.
This book aims to help you master the essential rules of grammar and punctuation by providing practical exercises for mastering the concepts commonly tested on the exam.

Why Grammar and Punctuation Matter for the Digital SAT

Grammar and punctuation are critical components of the Digital SAT, significantly impacting your performance in the Writing and Language section.
Unlike previous versions of the SAT, the Digital SAT focuses on how well you can apply grammar and punctuation rules in real-world contexts, emphasizing clarity and accuracy in communication. Mastering these skills not only prepares you for the test but also enhances your overall writing abilities.

Purpose of This Book

This book provides rigorous practice through targeted exercises designed to mirror the format and difficulty of the Digital SAT. With exercises covering everything from sentence structure to punctuation usage, this resource helps you practice efficiently under timed conditions, similar to the actual test environment.

Structure of the Book

The tests are divided into three sections, each targeting a specific aspect of grammar and punctuation mastery. The following concepts are tested;

Sentence Structure

- **Subject-Verb Agreement**: Ensuring that subjects and verbs agree in number (singular or plural).
- **Pronoun-Antecedent Agreement**: Ensuring that pronouns agree in number and gender with their antecedents.
- **Sentence Fragments and Run-ons**: Identifying and correcting incomplete sentences and run-on sentences.
- **Parallelism**: Using the same grammatical structure in lists and comparisons.
- **Modifier Placement**: Correctly placing descriptive words or phrases to avoid ambiguity or confusion.

Punctuation and Boundaries

- **Comma Usage**: Proper use of commas in lists, after introductory elements, and to separate clauses.
- **Semicolons and Colons**: Correct usage to connect independent clauses and to introduce lists or explanations.
- **Apostrophes**: Correct use in contractions and to show possession.
- **Quotation Marks**: Proper use with direct quotes and titles of short works.

Verb Usage

- **Verb Tense**: Consistency in verb tenses and correct usage of various tenses.
- **Verb Forms**: Correct forms of verbs, including irregular verbs.
- **Active vs. Passive Voice**: Preference for active voice over passive voice where appropriate.

Pronouns

- **Pronoun Case**: Correct use of subjective, objective, and possessive cases.
- **Ambiguous Pronouns**: Avoiding pronouns that do not clearly refer to a specific noun.

Agreement

- **Noun-Number Agreement**: Ensuring that nouns agree in number with other words in the sentence.
- **Pronoun Consistency**: Ensuring consistency in pronoun usage within a sentence or passage.

Usage

- **Word Choice**: Correct usage of commonly confused words (e.g., their/there/they're, affect/effect).
- **Idiomatic Expressions**: Proper usage of idiomatic phrases and prepositions.

Style and Rhetoric

- **Conciseness**: Eliminating wordiness and redundancy.
- **Tone and Style**: Ensuring that the tone and style are consistent and appropriate for the context.

Transitions

- **Addition**: moreover, furthermore, in addition
- **Contrast**: however, on the other hand, nevertheless
- **Cause and Effect**: therefore, as a result, consequently
- **Example**: for example, for instance, namely
- **Conclusion**: in conclusion, ultimately, in summary

Idioms

- **Contextual Understanding:** Idioms help test comprehension of phrases in context.
- **Avoid Literal Misinterpretation:** Knowing idioms prevents confusing literal and figurative meanings.
- **Language Fluency:** Idioms are key to demonstrating natural language use.
- **Correct Usage:** Mastery ensures accurate word choice and phrasing in the writing section.

How to Use This Book

This book contains 52 tests with <u>16 questions</u> each testing various aspects of Digital SAT Grammar and Punctuation. To maximize the benefits of this boo, you should **Practice Under Timed Conditions**.

Since the Digital SAT is a timed test, it's essential to practice completing each set within the <u>10-minute</u> time limit to build speed and accuracy.

This will not only help you excel in the Digital SAT but also in your future academic and professional endeavors.

Good luck, and may your efforts lead to success.

Test 1

A. Sentence Form and Structure
Select the choice that conforms to the conventions of Standard English.

1. The Constitution of the United States, written in 1787 by the Founding Fathers during the Constitutional Convention in Philadelphia, established a comprehensive framework for the federal government. Each state within the union, while maintaining a degree of autonomy and self-governance, must adhere to the fundamental principles _____.

A) has set forth by the Constitution

B) setting forth by the Constitution

C) set forth by the Constitution

D) had set forth by the Constitution

2. During the Industrial Revolution of the late 18th and early 19th centuries, technology significantly increased production capacity and efficiency. This transformative period marked a profound shift from predominantly agrarian societies to the _____ social structures and labor practices.

A) industrialized economies, fundamentally altering

B) industrializing economies, fundamentally altering

C) industrial economies, fundamentally altering

D) industry economies, fundamentally altering

3. The Gettysburg Address, delivered by President Abraham Lincoln on November 19, 1863, during the American Civil War, emphasized the principles of human equality. Lincoln's brief but powerful speech underscored the need for national unity and _____ a devastating conflict.

A) dedicating freedom in the face of

B) dedicated to freedom in the face of

C) dedicate to freedom in the face of

D) dedication to freedom in the face of

4. The Pulitzer Prize-winning novel *"To Kill a Mockingbird"* by Harper Lee, published in 1960, explores themes of racial injustice and moral growth in the Depression-era American South. The character of Atticus Finch, a principled lawyer and father, serves as a moral beacon throughout the narrative, _____ of empathy, integrity, and justice in a prejudiced society.

A) embody the values   B) embodying the values

C) embodies the values   D) embodied the values

5. The Harlem Renaissance, a cultural movement that flourished in the 1920s and 1930s in New York City's Harlem neighborhood, celebrated African American art, music, literature, and intellectual discourse. Influential figures like poet Langston Hughes and novelist Zora Neale Hurston played a crucial role in _____ and artistic expression.

A) defines this vibrant period of cultural awakening

B) defined period of cultural awakening

C) defining this vibrant period of cultural awakening

D) definition this vibrant period of cultural awakening

6. The Declaration of Independence formally declared the American colonies' freedom from British rule. This seminal document articulated the Enlightenment principles of natural rights and _____, laying the philosophical foundation for the new nation.

A) individual liberty   B) individuals liberty's

C) individuals liberty's   D) liberty of individuals

7. The civil rights movement of the 1950s and 1960s sought to end racial segregation and discrimination in the United States, particularly in the Jim Crow South. Prominent leaders like Dr. Martin Luther King Jr. advocated for nonviolent protest, civil disobedience, and _____ as a means to achieve social and legal reforms.

A) equal for all   B) equal to all

C) equality to all   D) equality for all

B. Transitions: Select the correct answer that completes the text with the most logical transition.

1. In the early 20th century, public health officials began recognizing the importance of sanitation in preventing disease. They launched numerous campaigns to educate the public about hygiene practices. _____ these efforts significantly reduced the spread of infectious diseases in urban areas.

A) Perhaps,   B) As a result,

C) Conversely,   D) Possibly,

2. During the Renaissance, artists sought to capture the natural world with greater realism. They studied human anatomy, experimented with perspective, and explored the effects of light and shadow. _____ their work began to reflect a more lifelike and three-dimensional quality.

A) On the contrary,   B) Excluding,

C) Therefore,   D) Dismissing,

3. The development of the internet has revolutionized communication. People can now connect instantly with others around the world, share information, and collaborate on projects. _____ it has also raised concerns about privacy and security.

A) Similarly,   B) Rejecting,

C) Fortunately,   D) Even now,

4. Ben Jonson's plays have transcended time, captivating audiences for centuries. His insightful exploration of human nature, richly developed characters, and masterful use of language ensure their continued relevance. _____ his works are studied in schools and universities worldwide, solidifying his place as a cornerstone of dramatic literature.

A) Moreover,   B) Nevertheless,

C) Conversely,   D) Instead,

5. Climate change is having a profound impact on global ecosystems. Rising temperatures are causing polar ice to melt, sea levels to rise, and weather patterns to become more extreme. _____ the efforts to mitigate climate change are increasingly focused on reducing carbon emissions and developing sustainable practices.

A) Similarly,   B) Consequently,

C) In contrast,   D) Even so,

6. The invention of the printing press in the 15th century was a turning point in history. It allowed for the mass production of books, making literature and knowledge more accessible to a wider audience. _____ it played a key role in the spread of the Renaissance and the Reformation.

A) Conversely,   B) All the same,

C) Therefore,   D) Nevertheless,

C. Punctuation & Boundaries: Select the correct answer from the options provided.

1. The project's success depended on several key factors: the team's ability to collaborate effectively, the availability of necessary resources, and _____ the stakeholders' commitment to the project's goals.

A) most importantly   B) most importantly,

C) most importantly;   D) most importantly:

2. After examining the evidence, the investigator concluded that the company's financial troubles were due to the CEO's mismanagement and the _____ failure to innovate.

A) employ"   B) employ

C) employees'   D) employees's

3. The famous line, "*To be or not to be, that is the question*," from Shakespeare's Hamlet, is often quoted to illustrate the complexity of human existence and _____.

A) meaning   B) meaning.

C) meaning,"   D) meaning".

Test 2

A. Sentence Form and Structure

Select the choice that conforms to the conventions of Standard English.

1. The Great Depression, which began with the stock market crash of October 1929, was the worst economic downturn in the history of the industrialized world. Lasting until the late 1930s, this severe economic contraction started after the collapse of stock prices on the New York Stock Exchange and _____, affecting millions worldwide.

A) led to widespread unemployment

B) led to widespread unemployments

C) led to widespread unemployed

D) led to widespread employ

2. The works of William Shakespeare remain profoundly influential in modern literature and theater. His plays, including tragedies like "*Hamlet*" and "*Macbeth*," comedies like "*A Midsummer Night's Dream*," and historical dramas like "*Henry V*," often explore complex characters and universal themes, _____.

A) making them timeless pieces of literary art

B) makes them timeless pieces of literature art

C) made them timeless pieces of literarily arts

D) make them timeless pieces of nonfiction

3. The Louisiana Purchase, completed in 1803 during Thomas Jefferson's presidency, nearly doubled the size of the young United States and provided valuable land for westward expansion. President Jefferson's administration negotiated the purchase with _____.

A) French's who was then ruled by Napoleon Bonaparte

B) French, who was then ruled by Napoleon Bonaparte

C) France's who was then ruled by Napoleon Bonaparte

D) France, who was then ruled by Napoleon Bonaparte

4. The theory of evolution by natural selection, proposed by British naturalist Charles Darwin in his 1859 book "*On the Origin of Species*," fundamentally changed the scientific understanding of biological diversity and the development of life on Earth. This groundbreaking theory posits that species evolve over time through _____, wherein organisms with favorable traits are more likely to survive and reproduce.

A) a process of selecting naturally

B) a process of nature selection

C) a process of natural selection

D) a process of natural select

5. The principle of _____ is a cornerstone of modern medical ethics, requiring healthcare providers to fully disclose the risks and benefits of any procedure before a patient agrees to treatment. This concept, which emerged in the mid-20th century, marked a significant shift away from the paternalistic approach that had previously dominated doctor-patient relationships.

A) informed concent   B) informed consent

C) inform concent   D) inform consent

6. In July 1969, NASA's Apollo 11 mission successfully landed astronauts Neil Armstrong and Buzz Aldrin on the moon, marking a _____ history and fulfilling President John F. Kennedy's goal of reaching the moon before the end of the 1960s.

A) major milestone in space

B) major milestone in space's

C) major milestone in spaced

D) major milestone in spaces'

7. The New Deal, introduced by President Franklin D. Roosevelt, aimed to provide relief, recovery, and reform during the Great Depression. Programs like the Civilian Conservation Corps and the Works Progress Administration were designed to _____.

A) creation jobs   B) create jobs

C) creates job   D) created jobs

B. Idioms

Select the correct answer from the options provided.

1. As the company's CEO prepared to sign the multimillion-dollar merger agreement, his assistant nervously handed him the pen. With a steady hand, he placed his _____ at the bottom of the document, sealing the deal that would change the course of both companies forever.

A) John Hancock

B) bull in a China shop

C) sail under false colors

D) heart in the right place

2. Sarah had always been a bit of a perfectionist, but her coworkers were starting to lose patience with her tendency to _____. When she spent an entire afternoon debating the shade of blue to use in a PowerPoint presentation, her team finally confronted her about her excessive attention to minor details.

A) Johnny on the spot

B) let the cat out of the bag

C) make a mountain out of a molehill

D) crack a book

3. As the deadline for his final exams approached, Tom realized he had fallen behind in his studies. Determined to catch up, he decided to _____ for the next two weeks, spending every available moment in the library and poring over his textbooks late into the night.

A) let someone slide

B) hit the books

C) grease monkey

D) quarrel with bread and butter

4. The rescue team had been searching for the lost hikers for days when they finally heard a faint distress call. Racing against the setting sun and dropping temperatures, they managed to locate and save the stranded group _____, just before a severe storm hit the area.

A) in the nick of time

B) on pins and needles

C) on the bandwagon

D) for a song

5. Julia had always trusted her best friend with her deepest secrets, but when she overheard Sarah sharing her confidential information with their mutual acquaintances, she felt as if she had received a _____. The betrayal left her questioning the foundation of their entire friendship

A) cast in the same mold

B) a bird's eye view

C) stab in the back

D) red herring

C. Missing Words: Select the correct answer from the options provided.

The Amazon rainforest is a vast and vibrant ecosystem, teeming with life in all its diverse forms. The towering trees form a thick canopy, (1) _____ (filtering, exuding, releasing, holding) most of the sunlight and creating a dappled, green twilight below. This dense foliage provides a (2) _____ (arid, humid, barren, desolate) environment, perfect for the survival of a multitude of exotic plants and animals.

Countless species of brightly colored birds flit through the branches, while hidden amongst the undergrowth, a variety of (3) _____ (reptiles, trawls, amphibians, amoeba) slither, crawl, and hop. Sadly, due to deforestation, this irreplaceable habitat is under threat, and efforts are underway to (4) _____ (pollute, dismantle, preserve, flatten) this vital ecosystem for future generations.

Test 3

A. Sentence Form and Structure

Select the choice that conforms to the conventions of Standard English.

1. The ancient Greek philosophers Socrates, Plato, and Aristotle _____ like ethics, metaphysics, epistemology, and political philosophy that continue to influence Western thought today. Their work laid the groundwork for many of the central questions and concepts that continue to be debated by philosophers and thinkers today.

A) develops foundational ideas in fields

B) has developed foundational ideas in fields

C) developed foundational ideas in fields

D) is developing foundational ideas in fields

2. The Impressionist painters, a group of 19th-century artists who rebelled against the strictures and conventions of the art academies, were known for _____ and unique approach to light and color.

A) its revolutionary

B) their revolutionary

C) his revolutionary

D) her revolutionary

3. The Great Wall of China, renowned for its historical significance and impressive length, attracts millions of visitors each year. _____ remains one of the most iconic landmarks in the world.

A) Known for its grandeur, the Great China Wall

B) The Great Wall of China stretches over 13,000 miles

C) Stretch over 13,000 miles, it

D) Grandeur over 13,000 miles, the Wall

4. The Roman Empire is often remembered for its numerous achievements and innovations in various fields. _____ These characteristics collectively underscore the empire's legacy of strength and sophistication.

A) The Roman Empire was known for its powerful army, advanced engineering, and they also had great architecture.

B) The Roman Empire was known for having a powerful army, as well as advanced engineering, and great architectural works.

C) The Roman Empire was known for its powerful army, for advanced engineering, and also had great architecture.

D) The Roman Empire was known for its powerful army, advanced engineering, and great architecture.

5. Exploring the excavation site, the archaeologist marveled at the numerous historical artifacts scattered around. The dig had already yielded several significant finds, but today brought an unexpected discovery. _____ The find provided invaluable insights into the daily lives of the site's ancient inhabitants.

A) Walking through the excavation site, the archaeologist discovered a pottery shard.

B) The archaeologist discovered a pottery shard walking through the excavation site

C) The archaeologist walking through the excavation site discovered a pottery shard.

D) A pottery shard was discovered by the archaeologist walking through, the excavation site

6. The Code of Hammurabi, an ancient Babylonian legal text, is one of the earliest known examples of written law. Discovered in 1901, _____ laws covering various aspects of Mesopotamian society.

A) it contains 282   B) its contains 282

C) it's contains 282   D) itself contains 282

7. In the heart of the bustling city, where the sounds of traffic _____ his thoughts, he found solace in a quiet corner café, sipping his coffee slowly and savoring the moment.

A) drowned out

B) were drowning out

C) had drowned out

D) drown out

B. Transitions: Select the correct answer that completes the text with the most logical transition.

1. Advances in medical technology have significantly improved patient outcomes. New diagnostic tools and treatments have made it possible to detect diseases earlier and manage chronic conditions more effectively. _____ there are still disparities in access to healthcare across different populations.

A) However,   B) Similarly,

C) Therefore,   D) Consequently,

2. The weather forecast predicted a day of torrential downpours, threatening to dampen the outdoor concert. _____ a sea of determined music lovers, armed with raincoats and umbrellas, gathered in the park, their enthusiasm undeterred by the possibility of getting soaked.

A) Conversely,   B) Moreover,

C) For example,   D) Nevertheless,

3. The initial clinical trials for the new medication yielded promising results, demonstrating a significant reduction in symptoms. _____ in-depth analysis of the data revealed minimal side effects, making it a potentially viable treatment option for a wide range of patients.

A) Still,   B) Consequently,

C) However,   D) Furthermore,

4. The Great Depression of the 1930s had a devastating impact on the global economy. Millions of people lost their jobs, and many businesses were forced to close. _____ governments around the world implemented policies to stabilize their economies and provide relief to those affected.

A) Consequently,   B) Conversely,

C) Nevertheless,   D) Contrarywise,

5. Some argue that increased automation in factories will lead to widespread unemployment. _____ it could also create a demand for a new kind of skilled worker – one adept at maintaining, repairing, and programming these complex machines, leading to a shift in the labor market rather than its complete collapse.

A) Conversely,   B) Even with,

C) Not really,   D) Exceedingly,

6. The bustling city center throbbed with life, a cacophony of car horns, street vendors hawking their wares, and excited chatter filling the air. _____ the tranquil mountain village, nestled amidst a hushed canopy of pine trees, offered a stark contrast to the hustle and bustle below. The only sounds were the soft whisper of the breeze through the needles and the distant, ethereal melody of chirping birds.

A) The same,   B) Likewise,

C) Contrarily,   D) Similarly,

C. Punctuation & Boundaries: Select the correct answer from the options provided.

1. _____teacher asked, "Who can explain the symbolism of the conch in *Lord of the Flies*?"

A) The   B) "The

C) The;   D) The"

2. The history textbook explored the _____ tomb, filled with treasures that hadn't been disturbed for centuries.

A) Pharaohs

B) Pharaoh's

C) Pharaohs"

D) Pharaohes"

3. Although the upcoming quiz focused heavily on the French _____ hours studying the intricacies of the Roman Republic, just in case.

A) Revolution; I spent

B) Revolution I spent,

C) Revolution I, spent

D) Revolution, I spent

Test 4

A. Sentence Form and Structure

Select the choice that conforms to the conventions of Standard English.

1. During the annual science fair, several students presented innovative projects. Among them was Maria, whose project on renewable energy sources received high praise. She _____ months before the science fair began, and her efforts were clear in her detailed presentation.

A) has been working on her project for

B) worked on her project for

C) had been working on her project for

D) works on her project for

2. During the annual school play, the students performed a scene from a famous Shakespearean drama. The performance was well-received by the audience. The lead actor _____ flawlessly, impressing everyone present.

A) recites his lines

B) reciting his lines

C) recite his lines

D) recited his lines

3. The HR department had a comprehensive training program in place. After every fresh hiring, _____ complete an orientation session.

A) new employees were required to

B) the new employee receive training

C) training provided was to the new employee

D) the employee was responsible for

4. During history class, the teacher asked John and _____ our project to the class. We had been working collaboratively on a research paper about the Roman Empire, and the teacher felt our presentation would be a great way to share our findings with our classmates.

A) us to present

B) my to present

C) me to present

D) myself to present

5. The committee, which consists of several experts in environmental science and urban planning, _____ proposal for the new community park. Their diverse expertise ensured a thorough evaluation of the plan's potential impact on the environment and the needs of the residents.

A) are responsible for reviewing the

B) is responsible for reviewing the

C) have responsible for reviewing the

D) were responsible for reviewing the

6. The Inuit people of Greenland have a rich oral tradition, and _____ shape-shifting creatures and spirits. These stories, passed down through generations, offer a glimpse into the Inuit worldview and their deep connection to the natural world.

A) its stories often features

B) his stories often features

C) their stories often feature

D) her stories often feature

7. The playwright, whose work _____ received numerous awards throughout his career. His ability to weave complex characters and compelling narratives captivated theatergoers, making each performance a memorable experience. From intimate dramas to grand epics, his plays, rich in language and emotion, continue to resonate with people of all ages.

A) had been admiring by audiences around the world,

B) was admiring by audiences around the world,

C) is admired by audiences around the world,

D) has been admired by audiences around the world,

B. Idioms

Select the correct answer from the options provided.

1. After retiring from his job as a French teacher, Robert realized his language skills were getting rusty. Determined to maintain his fluency, he decided to _____ his French by watching French films, reading French literature, and joining a local conversation group for Francophiles.

A) juggle frogs

B) air one's dirty laundry

C) show the door

D) brush up on

2. Living next door to a family with five energetic children and three large dogs was enough to _____. For the introverted writer who worked from home, the constant noise and commotion made it nearly impossible for her to concentrate on her latest novel.

A) take your medicine

B) go under the hammer

C) drive one crazy

D) bark up the wrong tree

3. The dedicated postal worker took pride in his commitment to delivering mail, _____, never letting adverse weather conditions or personal inconveniences interfere with his duty to ensure that every letter and package reached its intended recipient on time.

A) eat humble pie

B) batten down the hatches

C) rain or shine

D) walking on broken glass

4. As her daughter prepared to go on stage for her first leading role in the school play, Sarah hugged her tightly and whispered, "_____!" The young actress took a deep breath, feeling a mix of nervousness and excitement as she stepped into the spotlight.

A) you can't hide elephants in mouse holes

B) break a leg

C) black sheep of the family

D) nobody's fool

5. For years, the politician had managed to keep his past indiscretions hidden from the public eye. However, as he announced his candidacy for the presidency, he feared that the _____ might finally be exposed, potentially derailing his entire campaign and destroying the carefully crafted image he had built over decades

A) foot in mouth

B) skeletons in his closet

C) recipe for disaster

D) dances to the tune

C. Missing Words: Select the correct answer from the options provided.

The invention of the internet has revolutionized the way we live, work, and communicate. Before the internet, information was primarily accessed through libraries and physical media like books and newspapers. Research projects were time-consuming, often (1) _____ (relaxing, requiring, diminishing, unwinding) visits to multiple libraries and sifting through countless resources. However, with the advent of the internet, information became readily (2) _____ (available, inadequate, hidden, cryptic) at our fingertips.

The internet has facilitated (3) _____ (solitary, close, unrepeated, distant) communication, allowing us to connect with people across the globe through email, social media, and video conferencing. While the internet offers undeniable benefits, it's crucial to develop critical thinking skills to (4) _____ (condemn, evaluate, ignore, praise) the information we encounter online and be mindful of potential pitfalls like cyberbullying and misinformation. The internet's ever-evolving nature ensures it will continue to shape the way we interact with the world around us.

Test 5

A. Sentence Form and Structure

Select the choice that conforms to the conventions of Standard English.

1. Excerpt from a textbook passage: *"The Antikythera mechanism, an ancient Greek analog computer used to predict astronomical positions and eclipses, was discovered in a shipwreck off the Greek island of Antikythera. Despite its complexity, _____ until the development of mechanical astronomical clocks in the 14th century. "*

A) nothing come close to matching its sophistication

B) it remained unrivaled in it technological prowess

C) no similarly intricate device emerged

D) it was the coolest gadget around for centuries

2. William Shakespeare's sonnets, a collection of 14-line poems known for their intricate rhyme schemes and powerful imagery, _____ beauty, mortality, and the passage of time. These timeless themes, explored through rich metaphors and vivid language, resonate with readers even centuries after they were written.

A) explores universal themes of love,

B) explore universal themes of love,

C) exploring universal themes of love,

D) have been exploring universal themes of love,

3. The Magna Carta, a landmark document in the history of constitutional law, was agreed upon by King John of England in 1215. This charter of rights had _____ traditions of feudal law, influencing many legal systems that followed.

A) its roots in the longstanding

B) their roots in the longstanding

C) his roots in the longstanding

D) her roots in the longstanding

4. Leonardo da Vinci, the renowned Renaissance artist, is celebrated for creating the Mona Lisa, among other masterpieces. The most concise way to describe it is: "_____."

A) The Mona Lisa, which is a really famous painting, was created by Leonardo da Vinci.

B) The Mona Lisa, a famous painting, was created by Leonardo da Vinci.

C) The Mona Lisa is a very prominent painting. It was masterfully created by Leonardo da Vinci.

D) The Mona Lisa is a very famous painting it was created by Leonardo da Vinci a great artist.

5. The French Revolution, a pivotal period in history, was fundamentally _____. These ideals became the rallying cry for revolutionaries and symbolized their quest for a more just and equal society.

A) driven by a desire for liberty, equality, and as people wanted fraternity.

B) driven by a desire for liberty, equality, and for fraternity.

C) driven by a desire for liberty, equality, and fraternity.

D) driven by desiring liberty, equality, and wanting fraternity.

6. At the birthday celebration, all the guests were captivated by the intricately designed cake. The _____ was the highlight of the party, drawing admiration from everyone present.

A) beautiful with flowers

B) with flower beautifully

C) beautifully decorated cake with flowers

D) with flowers decorate beautifully

7. The Rosetta Stone, a granodiorite stele inscribed with three versions of a decree, was instrumental in deciphering Egyptian hieroglyphs. After years of study, _____ secrets of ancient Egyptian writing.

A) it unlocked the

B) them unlocked the

C) they unlocked the

D) its unlocked the

B. Transitions: Select the correct answer that completes the text with the most logical transition.

1. _____ the development of the printing press, books were copied by hand, which made them expensive and rare. Therefore, the invention of the printing press by Johannes Gutenberg revolutionized the availability of books and literacy rates across Europe.

A) Before

B) With this in mind,

C) Hence

D) For instance,

2. Despite the numerous benefits of exercising regularly, many people find it difficult to maintain a consistent workout routine. _____ they miss out on the physical and mental health benefits that come with regular exercise, ultimately impacting their overall well-being.

A) Consequently,

B) Accordingly,

C) Either way,

D) Meanwhile,

3. Given the rapid advancements in technology that are reshaping various sectors, industries are constantly evolving and adapting to new innovations. _____ this continuous change, workers must consistently update their skills to remain competitive in the ever-evolving job market.

A) In all honesty,

B) And so,

C) Whereas

D) Because of

4. _____ the benefits of renewable energy sources are widely recognized, transitioning from fossil fuels presents significant challenges. Nevertheless, many countries are investing heavily in renewable energy to combat climate change.

A) Much less

B) While

C) Conversely

D) Moreover

5. Although many people believe that money can buy happiness, studies have shown that after a certain point, increased wealth does not correlate with increased happiness. _____ the happiness of lottery winners often returns to its previous level within a few years, illustrating this paradox.

A) In the first place,

B) Consequently,

C) For instance,

D) Even more,

6. In addition to the undeniable importance of achieving academic success, extracurricular activities play a crucial role in a student's overall development by fostering a variety of essential life skills. _____ they provide valuable opportunities for students to develop social skills, collaborate with peers, and explore new interests outside the classroom.

A) Whatever happens,

B) Moreover,

C) In contrast,

D) Granting that,

C. Punctuation & Boundaries: Select the correct answer from the options provided.

1. A team of researchers studied the migratory patterns of two bird _____ the Arctic Tern, which travels the longest migration route, and the Ruby-throated Hummingbird, known for its rapid wing beats.

A) species.

B) species'

C) species-

D) species,

2. The biologists observed that the monarch butterfly does not use its vibrant colors to blend in with its surroundings' _____ the bright hues serve as a warning to predators about its toxicity.

A) colors, rather,

B) colors; rather;

C) colors: rather:

D) colors; rather,

3. A short-term economic forecast aims to project market trends for the next three to six _____ its scope is narrower than that of a long-term forecast, which covers several years.

A) months and

B) months, and'

C) months; and,

D) months; and.

Test 6

A. Sentence Form and Structure

Select the choice that conforms to the conventions of Standard English.

1. The Parthenon, an ancient Greek temple dedicated to the goddess Athena, stands atop the Acropolis in Athens. Despite centuries of damage and decay, _____ classical Greek culture.

A) its remains an iconic symbol in

B) them remains an iconic symbol in

C) it's remains an iconic symbol of

D) it remains an iconic symbol of

2. The Renaissance was a period of cultural rebirth in Europe. During this time, _____ produced numerous masterpieces that continue to inspire artists today. These artists, along with many others, broke away from the rigid styles of the Middle Ages and embraced a renewed interest in classical art, human anatomy, and perspective.

A) they rose to Leonardo da Vinci and Michelangelo

B) artists like Leonardo da Vinci and Michelangelo

C) it seems as if Leonardo da Vinci and Michelangelo

D) the period Leonardo da Vinci and Michelangelo

3. Last summer, our family took a trip to Yellowstone National Park. We were excited to explore the geysers and witness the diverse wildlife. By the time we reached the park, we _____ for over six hours without a break.

A) have driven   B) drove

C) had been driving   D) are driving

4. Extract from a Scientific Journal: *"In 1928, Alexander Fleming accidentally discovered penicillin when he noticed that mold growing on a contaminated culture plate had created a bacteria-free circle around itself. _____ led to the development of antibiotics, revolutionizing modern medicine. "*

A) This happy accident

B) This serendipitous observation

C) This lucky break

D) This totally random event.

5. In *A Tale of Two Cities*, Charles Dickens masterfully depicts the tumultuous period of the French Revolution. In the opening line, Dickens reflects on the contradictions of the era: *"It was the best of times, it was the worst of times."* _____ the complex nature of the age, highlighting both its promises and its perils.

A) Charles Dickens write that it was a time that had

B) Charles Dickens wrote about a time that had

C) Charles Dickens writing about a time that has

D) Charles Dickens is writing that it is a time that

6. In developing their marketing strategy, the team _____ to ensure they reach their target audience effectively. Analyzing customer feedback, sales trends, and market research will provide valuable insights. This comprehensive approach will help them craft campaigns that resonate with consumers.

A) must considered data from various sources

B) must considers data from various sources

C) must consider data from various sources

D) must be considered data from various sources

7. In order to meet the academic requirements of their course, the students must adhere to the submission deadlines. Each of the students _____ submit their assignments by Friday. This ensures fairness and allows the instructor to provide timely feedback.

A) are required to

B) is required to

C) have required to

D) were required to

B. Idioms

Select the correct answer from the options provided.

1. As a recent college graduate, James was excited to buy his first car. However, when he visited the dealership and saw the prices of the latest models with all the advanced features, he was shocked. Realizing that purchasing a brand-new vehicle would _____, James decided to look for a reliable used car instead.

A) burn the midnight oil

B) eleventh-hour decision

C) break the back of

D) cost an arm and a leg

2. Anna had been planning her dream vacation for months, meticulously researching destinations and booking accommodations. On the day before her departure, her best friend called with an exciting job opportunity that required an immediate interview. Her mother advised her to _____ and carefully consider her options before making a hasty decision.

A) get a slap on the wrist

B) kick up a row

C) hold her horses

D) ask for the moon

3. When Lisa saw her colleague's new designer handbag, she couldn't help but feel _____. She had been saving up for months to buy a similar one, but her colleague had received it as a gift from her wealthy aunt. Lisa tried to hide her feelings, but her friend could sense her jealousy.

A) green with envy

B) Jekyll and Hyde

C) a bit under the weather

D) shake a leg

4. Mark was an aspiring musician who practiced guitar for hours every day. His dedication to music was so intense that he often said he would _____ for the chance to perform on stage with his favorite rock band. His passion drove him to pursue his dreams relentlessly.

A) give his right arm

B) jog the memory

C) bet on the wrong horse

D) be on cloud nine

5. The constant noise from the construction site next door started to _____ Emily. She found it increasingly difficult to concentrate on her work from home, and the incessant drilling and hammering were affecting her sleep. Eventually, she decided to temporarily relocate to a quieter neighborhood.

A) fall on her sword

B) bug

C) vent her spleen

D) burn a hole in the pocket

C. Missing Words: Select the correct answer from the options provided.

The process of photosynthesis is crucial for life on Earth, as it allows plants to convert (1) _____ (darkness, sunlight, wind, water) into energy. This energy conversion is fundamental for the survival of the plant and, by extension, all living organisms that rely on plants directly or indirectly. Through this process, plants absorb carbon dioxide from the air and (2) _____ (catch, release, capture, ignore) oxygen, which is essential for most living organisms to breathe. The chlorophyll in plant cells plays a vital role in (3) _____ (reflecting, absorbing, scattering, deflecting) light energy, which is then used to convert water and carbon dioxide into glucose and oxygen.

This intricate system not only provides food for plants, enabling their growth and reproduction, but also (4) _____ (undermines, complicates, supports, rejects) the entire ecosystem by sustaining herbivores and, consequently, carnivores. By maintaining the balance of oxygen and carbon dioxide in the atmosphere, photosynthesis ensures the stability of the biosphere.

Test 7

A. Sentence Form and Structure

Select the choice that conforms to the conventions of Standard English.

1. The advent of digital technology has profoundly impacted various aspects of modern life. The rise of digital technology in the 21st century _____ significant transformations in communication, entertainment, and education.

A) bring about

B) brings about

C) has brought about

D) have brought about

2. In her autobiography, the famous author recounts the various stages of her literary career, from her early struggles to her eventual success. She _____ was only twenty-four, and it quickly became a bestseller.

A) publishes first her novel when she

B) published her first novel when she

C) had published her first novel when she

D) is publishing first her novel when she

3. The solution _____ was added, signaling the start of the reaction. Scientists observed the transformation with excitement, noting how the intensity of the color indicated the reaction's progress. This visual cue was crucial for monitoring the experiment effectively.

A) changes color to a vibrant blue when the catalyst

B) changing color to a vibrant blue when the catalyst,

C) had changes color to a vibrant blue when the catalyst,

D) changed color to a vibrant blue when the catalyst

4. In the shadow of the towering black pines, where the wind sighed mournfully through their branches, the travelers _____ The dense forest, shrouded in mist, seemed to whisper ancient secrets as they moved forward.

A) continues their journey.

B) continue their journey.

C) continued their journey.

D) are continuing their journey.

5. Between you and _____ is the best solution we have. We've both been brainstorming for a while, and this option seems to address all the key challenges most effectively.

A) we, I think this

B) mine, I think this

C) me, I think this

D) us, I think this

6. The Great Barrier Reef, one of the most remarkable natural wonders on Earth, is home to a diverse array of marine life. Its vibrant ecosystem and stunning scenery make it a prime destination for travelers and _____ tourists from around the world.

A) their beauty attracts

B) its beauty attracts

C) our beauty attracts

D) your beauty attracts

7. In short, the human circulatory system _____.

A) transports blood throughout the body, delivering oxygen and nutrients to cells and removing waste products.

B) the heart pumps blood through arteries, veins, and capillaries.

C) blood carries oxygen, nutrients, and waste products throughout the body.

D) the circulatory system is essential for human survival

B. Transitions: Select the correct answer that completes the text with the most logical transition.

1. _____ the beginning of the 21st century, the world has witnessed significant changes in communication technology. For example, the rise of social media platforms has transformed the way people interact and share information.

A) For this reason   B) Since

C) Hence   D) Then

2. Even though electric cars are becoming more popular, there are still many challenges to their widespread adoption. _____ the availability of charging infrastructure remains a major hurdle for many potential buyers.

A) Accordingly,   B) On the condition,

C) Yet,   D) In particular,

3. The impacts of the climate crisis are not only environmental but also economic and social. _____ it is imperative that we address these issues comprehensively to ensure a sustainable future.

A) Thus,   B) Either way,

C) Still,   D) Furthermore,

4. Given that education is a fundamental right, it is essential that governments ensure equal access to quality education for all citizens. _____ societal inequalities will continue to widen.

A) Otherwise,   B) Above all,

C) Conversely,   D) In contrast,

5. For example, cities around the world are implementing bike-sharing programs to reduce traffic congestion and promote sustainable transportation. _____ these programs encourage healthier lifestyles by providing an easy and accessible way to exercise.

A) To say nothing of,   B) Consequently,

C) Additionally,   D) Let alone,

6. _____ traditional marketing strategies rely heavily on print and broadcast media, digital marketing leverages online platforms and social media to reach a wider audience. Therefore, businesses must adapt their marketing approaches to stay relevant in the digital age.

A) In the first place   B) Whereas

C) In contrast   D) Alternatively

C. Punctuation & Boundaries: Select the correct answer from the options provided.

1. Given a newly purchased electronic device, Alex noticed the language options for the instruction manual. The instruction manual was printed in _____.

A) English/French

B) English,French

C) English-French

D) English"French

2. As she began to clarify her decision, she stated, "The reason I left is _____ "

A) because...

B) because!

C) because-

D) because'

3. In the article highlighting the latest advancements in the field, it was noted, _____

A) "The new technology is revolutionary".

B) "The new technology is revolutionary".

C) "The new technology is revolutionary"

D) "The new technology is revolutionary."

Test 8

A. Sentence Form and Structure

Select the choice that conforms to the conventions of Standard English.

1. Excerpt from a Scientific Journal: *"The Amazon Rainforest plays a crucial role in maintaining the planet's ecological balance. The Amazon Rainforest, a vast and biodiverse ecosystem spanning several countries in South America, _____ to preserve countless species and regulate the global climate. Protecting this vital region is essential for sustaining biodiversity and mitigating climate change. "*

A) serves as a critical habitat

B) acts as a natural barrier for animals

C) is a great place for wildlife

D) keeps the planet cool and green

2. The French Revolution was a period of significant social and political upheaval. During this time, _____ was overthrown, leading to dramatic changes in French society. The absolute power of the king was abolished, and a republic was established. This revolution had a profound impact not only on France but also on the course of European history.

A) the people

B) the monarchy, which had ruled France for centuries

C) its democratic government

D) the revolution

3. Recognizing the fatigue of his troops, the general took immediate action. _____.

A) Exhausted from the long march, the general ordered them to make camp

B) The general ordered them to make camp exhausted from the long march

C) They were ordered to make camp by the general exhausted from the long march

D) from the long march, they were exhausted ordered to make camp by the general

4. The Renaissance was characterized by _____.

A) a renewed interest in classical learning, artistic innovation, and scientific inquiry was pursued

B) a renewed interest in classical learning, artistic innovation, and the pursuit of scientific inquiry

C) renewing interest in classical learning, innovating artistically, and pursuing scientific inquiry

D) artistic, innovation, and scientific inquiry

5. After a long day at school, Sarah decided to take a walk in the park to clear her mind. However, the clouds began to gather ominously, threatening rain. _____ she quickly returned home.

A) As the storm was approaching,

B) She enjoyed the fresh air

C) The trees were swaying

D) The rain began to fall

6. Ancient Greece was a region made up of numerous independent city-states, each with _____. Some of the most famous city-states included Athens, Sparta, Corinth, and Thebes.

A) its own unique political and social structure

B) their own unique political and social structure

C) his own unique politics and social structure

D) her own unique politics and social structure

7. The theory of evolution by natural selection, proposed by Charles Darwin, _____ species change over time through the inheritance of genetic variations.

A) explain how

B) have explained how

C) explains how

D) are explaining how

B. Idioms

Select the correct answer from the options provided.

1. The research facility boasted _____ equipment for their groundbreaking experiments. Scientists from around the world were eager to collaborate with the team, knowing that they would have access to the most advanced technology available in their field.

A) a dish fit for Gods

B) state-of-the-art

C) in black and white

D) fool's paradise

2. When Tom's friends dared him to eat an entire extra-large pizza by himself, he confidently accepted the challenge, declaring that it would be _____. However, halfway through, he realized he had severely underestimated the difficulty of the task.

A) a piece of cake

B) graveyard shift

C) asleep at the switch

D) kangaroo court

3. The salesman's pitch seemed too good to be true, offering an amazing product at an unbelievably low price. Rachel was initially excited but then remembered her father's advice about being cautious with such offers. She decided not to _____ and instead did some research to verify the salesman's claims.

A) get her wires crossed

B) jam tomorrow

C) fall for it

D) break the silence

4. On the morning of his wedding day, Alex suddenly experienced _____. Despite months of planning and excitement, he found himself overwhelmed with doubt and anxiety. His best man had to reassure him that these feelings were normal and that he truly loved his fiancée.

A) cold feet

B) Davey Jones' locker

C) Johnny on the spot

D) zero tolerance

5. Living in the bustling city, Claire rarely had the opportunity to see a clear night sky. However, _____, when the power went out across the entire metropolitan area, she was able to witness a spectacular starry night from her balcony, reminding her of the beauty of the universe.

A) in the blues

B) to crow over

C) a witch hunt

D) once in a blue moon

C. Missing Words: Select the correct answer from the options provided.

The Renaissance was a period of significant cultural and intellectual revival in Europe, beginning in the 14th century. This era marked a departure from the Middle Ages, characterized by a renewed interest in classical Greek and Roman thought. Artists like Leonardo da Vinci and Michelangelo were known for their (1) _____ (innovative, outdated, simple, abstract) approaches to art, which emphasized realism and human emotion. This era also saw advancements in (2) _____ (alchemy, science, superstition, mythology), with figures such as Galileo challenging traditional views of the universe.

The invention of the printing press in the 15th century (3) _____ (hindered, simplified, revolutionized, complicated) the spread of knowledge, allowing ideas to circulate more widely. This technological breakthrough facilitated the circulation of books, pamphlets, and other printed materials, contributing to the growth of literacy and the exchange of ideas across Europe. Ultimately, the Renaissance laid the groundwork for the (4) _____ (primitive, modern, ancient, futuristic) world we know today.

Test 9

A. Sentence Form and Structure

Select the choice that conforms to the conventions of Standard English.

1. The 1930s were marked by significant historical events that had a profound impact on the United States. The Great Depression and the Dust Bowl of the 1930s _____ environmental devastation in the United States.

A) causes severe economical hardship and

B) has caused severe economical hardship and

C) cause severe economic hardship and

D) caused severe economic hardship and

2. The Maasai tribe of East Africa is known for _____. The Maasai people, renowned for their rich cultural heritage, have a deep connection to their land and their traditions.

A) their distinct clothing and elaborate beadwork

B) it's distinctive clothing and elaborate beadwork

C) his distinct clothing and elaborate beadwork

D) her distinctive clothing and elaborate beadwork

3. To be concise, William Shakespeare, _____

A) born in Stratford-upon-Avon, is considered one of the greatest English playwrights.

B) who was born in Stratford-upon-Avon is widely regarded as ones of the greatest playwrights in the English language

C) born in Stratford-upon-Avon, is regard by many as one of the greatest playwrights who wrote in the English language.

D) whose birthplace was Stratford-upon-Avon, is widely consider to be one of the greatest playwrights in the history of the English language.

4. Excerpt from a University Magazine: *The Nazca Lines, a group of geoglyphs in southern Peru, were created between 500 BCE and 500 CE. These enormous ground drawings, _____, have puzzled researchers for decades.*

A) which are totally mind-blowing

B) that look like they were made by aliens

C) visible only from the air

D) whose purpose remains enigmatic

5. The town's annual marathon is a major event, attracting runners from all over the country. This year, the organizers made several changes to improve the experience for participants. By the time the race started, the volunteers _____ the route.

A) have set up water stations along

B) set up water stations along

C) had set up water stations along

D) are setting up water stations along

6. After an exhaustive physical examination that lasted for hours, I emerged feeling as if I _____ with a hundred probes and _____ with a hundred needles.

A) was poked relentlessly / was stabbed intensively

B) had been poked thoroughly / stabbed repeatedly

C) had been poked extensively / they stabbed me mercilessly

D) they poked me incessantly / I was stabbed continuously

7. The team of researchers _____ the conference. The scholars, comprised of experts from various fields, conducted extensive research on the topic and shared their valuable insights with the academic community at the conference.

A) has presented their findings at

B) have presented their finding at

C) was presented their finding at

D) is presented their findings at

B. Transitions: Select the correct answer that completes the text with the most logical transition.

1. _____ the heavy rain, the festival continued as planned, drawing crowds eager to enjoy the music and festivities. Vendors set up their booths under colorful tarps, and laughter filled the air as people danced in the puddles. The spirit of the event remained unshaken, showcasing the community's resilience.

A) Despite
B) So much so that
C) Because of this
D) Thus

2. _____ urban areas, rural communities often face unique challenges in accessing healthcare services. As a result, residents of rural areas may experience poorer health outcomes compared to their urban counterparts.

A) On the condition that
B) In contrast to,
C) Therefore,
D) With this in mind,

3. Although technological advancements have greatly improved our quality of life, they have also introduced new ethical dilemmas. _____ the rise of artificial intelligence raises questions about privacy, job displacement, and the potential for biased algorithms.

A) For instance,
B) Luckily,
C) Granting that,
D) In contrast,

4. The global population continues to grow, placing increased pressure on natural resources. _____, we must develop sustainable practices to ensure the long-term health of our planet.

A) In the event that,
B) Nevertheless,
C) Meanwhile,
D) For this reason,

5. Due to the interconnected nature of the global economy, financial crises in one country can have far-reaching effects. _____ the 2008 financial crisis, which began in the United States, quickly spread to other parts of the world, leading to a global recession.

A) With this in mind,
B) Despite,
C) In contrast,
D) For example,

6. _____ art is often seen as a form of personal expression, it also plays a significant role in cultural preservation. Thus, art helps to maintain and celebrate the heritage and traditions of different communities.

A) In either event
B) Though
C) And if
D) Whichever happens

C. Punctuation & Boundaries: Select the correct answer from the options provided.

1. After months of planning and community input, the _____ playground in the local park was recently renovated to provide a safer and more enjoyable space for kids.

A) childrens
B) children's
C) childrens"
D) childrens's

2. During the press conference, the reporter noted, "*The new policy _____ will impact all employees, ensuring fairness and transparency in the workplace.*"

A) (effective January 1,
B) [effective January 1]
C) effective January, 1
D) effective January 1}

3. I was going to tell you about my trip to Italy, but _____ I think I'll save the details for another time. It was an adventure I'll never forget.

A) ,
B) ;
C) ...
D) .

Test 10

A. Sentence Form and Structure

Select the choice that conforms to the conventions of Standard English.

1. In classical literature, numerous poets relied on their audiences for support. The presence and feedback of these audiences were crucial, as _____ for their work. Understanding this relationship helps to appreciate the significance of audience interaction in the development of literary works.

A) its provided validation and inspire

B) we provided validation and inspiration

C) they provided validation and inspiration

D) us provided validation and inspire

2. Several initiatives were _____ to combat climate change and promote sustainability. These programs aim to reduce carbon emissions and encourage renewable energy use. By collaborating on global strategies, nations hope to create a healthier planet for future generations.

A) launched by governments worldwide

B) launch by governments worldwide

C) launching by governments worldwide

D) being launch by governments worldwide

3. In the operating room, _____ to ensure every detail is addressed before the procedure begins.

A) skilled surgeons and experienced nurses execute a comprehensive checklist

B) a detailed executed checklist is by trained doctors

C) a checklist is prepared by thorough experts

D) skilled practitioners' extensive checklist is carefully reviewed

4. The team, composed of students from diverse academic backgrounds, collaborated effectively to produce an exceptional project. _____ the introduction, while John worked on the conclusion. Their combined efforts resulted in a comprehensive and well-structured report that was well-received by the audience.

A) Maria writes   B) Maria writing

C) Maria wrote   D) Maria write

5. Through the looking-glass, Alice could see the enchanting garden, a place she _____ fateful day when she first stumbled into Wonderland. Its beauty was a stark contrast to the bizarre and chaotic world she had just navigated.

A) had longed to visit ever since that

B) longs to visit ever since that

C) was longing to visit ever since that

D) has longed to visit ever since that

6. The explorers _____ after months of navigating unfamiliar waters. Their detailed maps revealed rich landscapes and potential resources, sparking interest from nations eager to claim new territories. This discovery marked a significant turning point in the age of exploration.

A) were charting the new continent

B) have charted the new continent

C) had charted the new continent

D) will chart the new continent

7. The Ottoman Empire was known for its _____

A) strength of military, cultural diversity, and they had advanced administration systems.

B) military strength, cultural diversity, and advanced administration systems.

C) being strong militarily, having diverse culture, and systems of administration that were advanced.

D) strength in military, diversity of culture, and systems for administrating that were advanced.

B. Idioms

Select the correct answer from the options provided.

1. As a young entrepreneur, Sophia decided to _____ by launching a sustainable fashion brand in an industry known for its wasteful practices. Despite facing skepticism from traditional retailers, she remained committed to her eco-friendly vision and slowly began to change consumer perceptions.

A) give a piece of her mind

B) zip it

C) French leave

D) go against the grain

2. Inspired by her grandmother's successful career in medicine, Maria chose to _____ and pursue a degree in neuroscience. She often found herself reflecting on the challenges her grandmother must have faced as a woman in a male-dominated field decades ago.

A) follow in the footsteps

B) face the music

C) be on the edge

D) rake her over the coals

3. In the age of digital communication, John felt that important discussions were best held _____. He believed that nuances in facial expressions and body language were crucial for effective communication, especially when addressing sensitive topics with his team.

A) wrench in the works

B) face-to-face

C) like a sitting duck

D) Johnny-come-lately

4. At the company's annual retreat, the new manager organized a series of team-building exercises to _____ among the employees from different departments. The activities helped create a more relaxed atmosphere and encouraged interaction between colleagues who had never spoken before.

A) have an egg on the face

B) take a back seat

C) carry coals to new castle

D) break the ice

5. The sudden appearance of a giant spider in her bathroom _____ Sarah. She let out a blood-curdling scream that woke up her entire family, who came running to see what had happened.

A) blue in the face

B) appear out of now here

C) scared the living daylights out of

D) volte-face

C. Missing Words: Select the correct answer from the options provided.

In the field of psychology, the concept of cognitive dissonance plays a crucial role in understanding human behavior. It refers to the mental discomfort experienced when an individual holds (1) _____ (similar, supportive, contradictory, consistent) beliefs or attitudes. This internal conflict can arise when a person's actions, thoughts, or values don't align, creating a sense of imbalance. For instance, a person who smokes may feel (2) _____ (guilt, pride, indifference, satisfaction) about their health choices because they know the risks.

To alleviate this discomfort, individuals often (3) _____ (justify, ignore, confront, rationalize) their actions, leading to changes in beliefs or behaviors. They may downplay the negative consequences of smoking, emphasize the positive aspects, or even shift their overall attitude towards health. This phenomenon illustrates the (4) _____ (simplicity, complexity, predictability, variability) of human decision-making and the lengths to which people will go to maintain internal consistency and reduce psychological tension.

Test 11

A. Sentence Form and Structure

Select the choice that conforms to the conventions of Standard English.

1. _____ her exhibition attracted a large crowd. Many fans eagerly lined up to see her latest works, showcasing her unique style and innovative techniques. The atmosphere buzzed with excitement as attendees discussed the impact of her art.

A) The artist was well-known, therefore

B) But if they were tired,

C) It was already really late, so

D) And if so was thought,

2. Both Claude Monet and Pierre-Auguste Renoir were influential figures in the Impressionist movement, each with a unique approach to art. Neither Monet nor Renoir compromised _____, demonstrating their commitment to personal style and creative expression. This dedication contributed to their lasting impact on the art world.

A) their artistic vision

B) our artistic visions

C) her artistic vision

D) its artistic visions

3. The United Nations plays a vital role on the global stage, addressing various international challenges. The United Nations, an international organization founded in 1945, _____ international peace and security and promote cooperation among nations. Its ongoing efforts reflect its commitment to fostering global stability and collaboration.

A) work to maintain

B) have worked to maintain

C) working to maintain

D) works to maintain

4. Excerpt from a Motivational Speech: *"The journey is going to be tough, but you will get through_____*

A) "You guys should try harder, or you'll fail."

B) "Believe in yourself, and you'll be unstoppable!"

C) "I think you can do it, if you really try."

D) "You might be able to do it, but no promises."

5. Although the weather _____ pressed on with their journey, their breath visible in the crisp morning air. The path ahead was treacherous, but they were determined to reach their destination. Each step brought them closer to the summit, where they hoped to find shelter from the chilling winds.

A) got cold, the traveler's

B) was getting colder, the travelers

C) is getting colder, the travelers'

D) gets cold, the traveler

6. The Andean condor, with _____ wingspan, which can reach up to 10 feet, soars effortlessly over the towering peaks of the Andes Mountains in South America.

A) its impressive

B) them impressive

C) his impressive

D) her impressive

7. The community leader _____ of urban development at the upcoming town hall meeting. Residents are eager to hear about potential projects and how they might impact the neighborhood. This dialogue aims to foster collaboration and ensure that everyone's voice is heard.

A) are invited to discuss the future

B) is invited to discuss the future

C) had invited to discuss the future

D) were invited to discuss the future

B. Transitions: Select the correct answer that completes the text with the most logical transition.

1. The advancements in medical research have led to the development of new treatments and therapies. _____ many diseases that were once considered fatal are now manageable or even curable.

A) Nevertheless,   B) Anyhow,

C) Consequently,   D) Granting that,

2. _____ the significant progress made in gender equality, there are still many areas where disparities persist. For example, women continue to be underrepresented in leadership positions in many industries.

A) That being the case   B) In spite of

C) With this in mind   D) Meanwhile

3. _____ discussing the impact of global warming, it is important to consider both short-term and long-term effects. For instance, while extreme weather events have immediate consequences, rising sea levels represent a longer-term threat to coastal communities.

A) When   B) Secondly

C) However   D) By the way

4. Cultural diversity enriches societies by bringing in a variety of perspectives and experiences. _____ fostering an inclusive environment is beneficial for both individuals and communities as a whole.

A) To begin with,   B) Nevertheless,

C) Unfortunately,   D) Therefore,

5. Before the widespread use of antibiotics, many bacterial infections were often fatal. _____ the discovery of penicillin marked a turning point in medical history, significantly reducing mortality rates from bacterial infections.

A) Analogously,   B) Originally,

C) But even so,   D) For this reason,

6. _____ the internet provides access to vast amounts of information, digital literacy is an essential skill in today's world. Without it, individuals may struggle to navigate and critically evaluate online content.

A) Finally,   B) Given that

C) In all honesty,   D) After this

C. Punctuation & Boundaries: Select the correct answer from the options provided.

1. The author _____ will be giving a lecture tonight, sharing insights from their award-winning work and discussing the writing process, which has captivated readers and critics alike.

A) [who won the Pulitzer Prize-

B) who, won the Pulitzer Prize.

C) (who won the Pulitzer Prize)

D) {who won, the Pulitzer Prize}

2. During the summer months, families often take vacations, explore new places _____ time together, creating lasting memories and strengthening their bonds.

A) : and spend

B) , and spend

C) ... and spend

D) - and spend

3. The class debated whether Holden Caulfield in _____ Catcher in the Rye" is a reliable narrator, examining his perspective and the implications of his storytelling on the overall narrative.

A) "The

B) "The.

C) The

D) The"

Test 12

A. Sentence Form and Structure
Select the choice that conforms to the conventions of Standard English.

1. Sarah and _____ store to buy some groceries for the party. They made a list of necessary items, including chips, drinks, and party favors. We needed to stock up on chips, drinks, and other snacks to ensure there would be plenty for our guests.

A) me, went to the

B) myself went to the

C) I went to the

D) mine went to the

2. When the call finally _____, the sound of her voice was almost unrecognizable, distorted by the distance and the poor connection. Despite this, it brought an immense relief that could not be put into words.

A) came through

B) comes through

C) had come through

D) is coming through

3. At the art gallery, visitors admired the various paintings and sculptures on display. Each piece told a unique story. One of the paintings _____ with mountains and a river, evoking a sense of peace and tranquility. The artist skillfully captured the tranquility of the scene, using soft colors and delicate brushstrokes.

A) depict serene landscapes

B) depicts serene landscapes

C) depicted a serene landscape

D) depicting a serene landscape

4. As the sun began to set over the horizon, casting a warm golden glow across the water, the elegant swan _____ beneath the surface, leaving behind a ripple that shimmered in the fading light, much to the delight of the onlookers gathered along the shore.

A) had sink down

B) sinks gently

C) had sank quietly

D) sank gracefully

5. The Dead Sea Scrolls, ancient manuscripts discovered in the Qumran Caves, provide invaluable insights into ancient Judaism. Since _____ pored over these texts to better understand the development of religious thought and the beliefs of the people who created them.

A) its discovery in 1947, scholars had

B) their discovery in 1947, scholars have

C) it's discovery in 1947, scholars have

D) there discovery in 1947, scholars had

6. The Reformation sought to _____.

A) reforming the Catholic Church, promote literacy, and the translation of the Bible into vernacular languages.

B) reform the Catholic Church, to promote literacy, and translating the Bible into vernacular languages.

C) reform the Catholic Church, promote literacy, and translate the Bible into vernacular languages.

D) reforming the Catholic Church, literacy promotion, and the Bible's translation into vernacular languages.

7. During the summer vacation, Jason intended to read several classic novels. He had made a list of titles to tackle. _____ he only managed to finish one book.

A) Even though he was busy,

B) But he enjoyed each one,

C) Yet he found time,

D) Despite his best efforts,

B. Idioms

Select the correct answer from the options provided.

1. After losing touch with his childhood friend for several years, Mike decided to _____ and reconnect. He sent a heartfelt email reminiscing about their shared memories and expressing his hope to catch up soon.

A) flash in the pan

B) make his bed and lie on it

C) talk turkey

D) drop him a line

2. The professor's lecture on the ethical implications of artificial intelligence provided plenty of _____ for the students. Many left the class engaged in deep discussions about the potential consequences of advanced AI on society and human relationships.

A) food for thought

B) jobs for the boys

C) uncharted waters

D) salt on the earth

3. During the team meeting, when she pointed out the main issue causing the project's delays, she truly _____, prompting everyone to reconsider their strategies and work more effectively towards a solution.

A) had her hands full

B) be bouncing off the walls

C) waited for a raindrop in the drought

D) hit the nail on the head

4. When the elderly woman struggled to carry her groceries up the stairs, Mark didn't hesitate to _____. He offered to help her with the heavy bags, demonstrating that small acts of kindness can make a big difference in someone's day.

A) jump down her throat

B) lend her a hand

C) bring home the bacon

D) jump the gun

5. After a series of professional setbacks, Lisa decided it was time for a _____. She moved to a new city, changed careers, and embraced the opportunity to reinvent herself without the burden of past mistakes weighing her down.

A) clean slate

B) jump through hoops

C) judge, jury, and executioner

D) yellow-bellied

C. Missing Words: Select the correct answer from the options provided.

In the domain of philosophy, existentialism examines the nature of existence and the meaning of life. Prominent thinkers like Jean-Paul Sartre and Simone de Beauvoir argued that individuals must (1) _____ (inherit, ignore, deny, create) their own essence through choices and actions. This school of thought emphasizes the inherent (2) _____ (restriction, freedom, obligation, limitation) of individuals to define their own lives.

However, with this freedom comes the burden of (3) _____ (apathy, negligence, responsibility, indifference) for one's decisions. Ultimately, existentialism challenges people to confront the (4) _____ (clarity, absurdity, simplicity, predictability) of life and to find personal meaning in a chaotic world.

Test 13

A. Sentence Form and Structure
Select the choice that conforms to the conventions of Standard English.

1. The scientist's research, which _____, has significantly contributed to the field of renewable energy. Her groundbreaking work on sustainable resources is now a cornerstone in environmental studies.

A) was conducted over the last decades

B) has been conducted over the last decades

C) is conducted over the last decade

D) had been conducted over the last decade

2. Maria loves to bake, often experimenting with new recipes. She found an interesting recipe online for a chocolate soufflé. _____ she decided to make it for her friends.

A) The ingredients were expensive,

B) It seemed too complicated,

C) Even though it was a challenge,

D) Everyone enjoys chocolate,

3. The shift from a nomadic existence to a more settled way of life involved _____, all of which contributed to the rise of civilization and allowed people to thrive in one location.

A) humans started to settle in permanent communities

B) developing agriculture, domesticating animals, and establishing permanent communities

C) the domestication of animals to make fur

D) agriculture development, animals, and communities domestic

4. For the prestigious research program, the selection committee made it clear that they would admit _____, those who not only met the rigorous academic standards but also had extensive field experience and a proven track record of innovative contributions to their respective disciplines.

A) only highly qualified applicant

B) highly qualified only applicant

C) only the highly qualified applicants

D) the highly qualified only applicants

5. The Hanging Gardens of Babylon, one of the Seven Wonders of the Ancient World, were said to be a marvel of engineering and beauty. Although no archaeological evidence has been found, _____ the imagination of historians and the public alike.

A) its continue to captivate

B) they continue to captivate

C) its continued to captivate

D) them continue to captivate

6. As governments around the world implement stricter emissions regulations and consumers become increasingly aware of environmental issues, the demand for _____ has surged dramatically, prompting automakers to invest heavily in research and development.

A) it meant to

B) electric vehicles

C) the concept caught on,

D) the cars on the road

7. The artist, who _____ the essence of light in her paintings, has gained international recognition for her ability to transform ordinary scenes into luminous masterpieces that evoke emotion and wonder.

A) is striving tirelessly to captured

B) strives tirelessly to capture

C) had strived tirelessly to capture

D) has strived tirelessly to captured

B. Transitions: Select the correct answer that completes the text with the most logical transition.

1. The concept of metafiction in postmodern literature allows authors to play with the boundaries between fiction and reality. _____, it often serves to critique traditional narrative forms and conventions.

A) Perhaps   B) Conceivably

C) Nor   D) However

2. Social media has expanded the reach of contemporary poetry by allowing poets to connect with global audiences. _____, it has also changed how poems are written and consumed, often favoring shorter, more shareable content.

A) What is more   B) Or

C) In the first place D) Maybe

3. The portrayal of mental health in young adult fiction provides readers with relatable characters and situations. _____, it helps destigmatize mental health issues among young people.

A) In fact   B) Furthermore

C) But   D) Nor

4. George Orwell's "*Animal Farm*" is a powerful allegory for the corruption of socialist ideals in the Soviet Union. _____, the characters and events represent real historical figures and occurrences.

A) Unimaginably   B) As well as

C) Perhaps   D) In fact

5. The unreliable narrator in a mystery novel keeps readers guessing about the truth of the story. _____, this technique adds layers of complexity and intrigue to the narrative.

A) Additionally   B) Uncertainly

C) Doubtfully   D) To say nothing of

6. The COVID-19 pandemic precipitated a global economic upheaval, disrupting supply chains, and causing widespread shortages and price increases. These disruptions disproportionately impacted vulnerable populations, exacerbating existing economic inequalities. _____, the pandemic exposed the fragility of globalized systems and underscored the need for more resilient and equitable economic models.

A) In opposition   B) Moreover

C) On the other hand   D) Conversely

C. Punctuation & Boundaries: Select the correct answer from the options provided.

1. His voice trailed off as he contemplated the situation, and he finally murmured, "I don't know _____ The uncertainty in his tone was palpable, leaving everyone in the room waiting for more clarity.

A) what to do…   B) what to do…"

C) what to do!   D) what to do.

2. The meeting will take place on Monday _____ Tuesday, allowing for flexibility in scheduling among the participants. This approach ensures that everyone can be accommodated, whether they are available on one day or the other.

A) and/or   B) or/and

C) or/   D) and,

3. It was a perfect evening for a hike, with the sun setting beautifully and a gentle breeze in the air. The sky was painted in hues of orange and _____ it an ideal time to explore the trails.

A) pink; making   B) pink-making

C) pink, making   D) pink: making

Test 14

A. Sentence Form and Structure

Select the choice that conforms to the conventions of Standard English.

1. During the summer camp, the children participated in a variety of outdoor activities designed to foster a love for nature and teamwork. They especially enjoyed the nature hikes, where they explored the beauty of the wilderness together. Every morning, the group _____, discovering unique plants and wildlife along the way.

A) explores a new trail into forest

B) explored a new trail in the forest

C) exploring a new trail into forest

D) explore a new trail in the forest

2. Excerpt from a technical manual: *"This is the guide to fixing a faulty modem _____*

A) 'so, like, to fix this thing, you need to do this and that."

B) "Fixing this thing is pretty easy, just wing it..."

C) "You'll need to, um, try to figure out how to fix it yourself."

D) To repair the device, follow these steps: ..."

3. The international summit, which included representatives from multiple countries, _____ to the region by addressing longstanding conflicts and fostering dialogue among the involved parties.

A) has aim to bring peace

B) had aimed to bring peace

C) was aiming to bring peace

D) aim to bring peace

4. In the field of epigenetics, researchers explore how environmental factors can influence gene expression without altering _____. This fascinating area of study reveals the intricate relationship between genetics and the environment.

A) its underlying DNA sequence

B) their underlying DNA sequence

C) our underlying DNA sequence

D) his underlying DNA sequence

5. Her extensive experience and strong communication skills enabled _____ the team effectively, inspiring confidence and collaboration among all members as they worked towards their common goals.

A) she to lead

B) hers to lead

C) herself to lead

D) her to lead

6. During the seminar on renewable energy, the complex process of solar panel installation _____, ensuring that all participants understood the technical aspects required for effective implementation, while the importance of safety protocols was _____ to prevent any potential hazards during the installation process.

A) was explained thoroughly / taken diligently

B) explained masterfully / meticulously taken

C) was explained passionately / the students conscientiously take

D) the explained eloquently / were took enthusiastically

7. The concert was scheduled to start at 7 PM. The crowd began to gather outside the venue, excitement buzzing in the air. _____ the doors did not open until 7:30 PM.

A) Although everyone was eager,

B) They were disappointed,

C) The band was still warming up,

D) Many left early,

B. Idioms

Select the correct answer from the options provided.

1. I hadn't seen him _____; it felt like an eternity since our last encounter. The world had changed dramatically in that time. It was as if we were both living in different realities, yet we were still out of touch.

A) out of touch

B) on the same page

C) in ages

D) in two minds

2. Despite working two jobs and cutting back on luxuries, she still struggled to _____ each month, balancing the rising costs of rent and groceries while trying to save for her children's education.

A) have more money than sense

B) living high on the hog

C) roll in dough

D) make ends meet

3. The company is transitioning to a new customer relationship management system, so it's essential that all employees _____ to ensure a smooth transition. Those who resist change may find it challenging to adapt.

A) fall behind the times

B) get with the program

C) think outside the box

D) miss the boat

4. Having lived in the city for over a decade, she knew its streets, parks, and hidden gems _____, allowing her to navigate even the most complicated routes with ease and confidence.

A) like the back of her hand

B) living daylights

C) at the drop of a hat

D) in the blink of an eye

5. The newly renovated kitchen was _____, with gleaming countertops, polished appliances, and not a speck of dust in sight. It was a dream for anyone who loved to cook.

A) a sight for sore eyes

B) a hot mess

C) in shambles

D) spick and span

C. Missing Words: Select the correct answer from the options provided.

Personality theories in psychology provide a framework for understanding the complexities of human behavior and character. One prominent theory, the trait theory, suggests that personality is composed of (1) _____ (fixed, dynamic, stable, random) traits that influence how individuals respond to various situations. Another approach, known as the psychodynamic theory, emphasizes the role of unconscious processes and early life experiences in shaping personality, indicating that many individuals may be (2) _____ (aware, oblivious, indifferent, conscious) of the factors influencing their behavior.

Additionally, humanistic theories propose that individuals possess an inherent drive toward (3) _____ (self-actualization, conformity, isolation, regression) and personal growth, highlighting the importance of personal agency and fulfillment. Lastly, social-cognitive theories focus on the interaction between personal factors and environmental influences, suggesting that behavior is often a (4) _____ (reflection, consequence, contradiction, distraction) of both internal beliefs and external circumstances.

Test 15

A. Sentence Form and Structure
Select the choice that conforms to the conventions of Standard English.

1. The periodic table of elements, developed by Dmitri Mendeleev in the 19th century as a crucial tool for chemists, _____ according to their atomic structure and properties.

A) organizes the chemical elements

B) organize the chemical element

C) is organizing the chemical elements

D) have organized the chemical element

2. As the colonies sought to break free from British rule, they aimed to create a system that reflected their values and aspirations. The American Revolution was fought for _____.

A) to establish a new government, and for individual liberties.

B) independence, establish a new government, and they wanted individual liberties.

C) the establishment of a new government and the protection of individual liberties.

D) gain independence, a new government was to be established, and individual liberties.

3. As the scientist presented her groundbreaking findings at the conference, the audience listened intently, captivated by the implications of her research on climate change. Despite the intricacy of the subject matter, the atmosphere was charged with curiosity. _____ many attendees asked questions during the Q&A session.

A) While they were curious, but

B) This was unexpected, so

C) Their engagement was evident, as

D) The topic was not complex,

4. As the tourists wandered through the historic district, they found themselves captivated by the charm of the area. They got lost in _____ streets of the old city.

A) the winding, narrow

B) winding narrow,

C) narrow, the winding

D) the narrow, winding

5. Excerpt from a self-help blog: *"I'm sure you are at a point in life where you might be seeking a guiding voice _____*

A) "I'm an expert, so you should listen to me about this topic."

B) "I've been there, done that, and learned a thing or two."

C) "Let me tell you, this is how it is, and you should agree."

D) "I'm not sure, but I think this might be true."

6. To be concise, the concept of supply and demand in economics _____

A) is an economic model of price determination in a market, where the price for a good or service is base on the interaction between the supply of and demand for that good or service.

B) determines market prices through the interaction of product availability and consumer desire.

C) refers to the relationship between the available of a product or service and the desire for it among consumers, which together determine the price.

D) explains how the price of good and services in a market is determined by the interaction between the availability of those items (supply) and the desire for them among consumers (demand).

7. The geoglyphs in Peru, visible only from above, continue to puzzle archaeologists regarding _____ and the method of creation.

A) their purpose   B) her purpose

C) our purpose   D) its purpose

B. Transitions: Select the correct answer that completes the text with the most logical transition.

1. Microplastics have been found in various marine species, including fish and shellfish, posing a serious threat to their health and well-being. _____, these tiny pollutants can inadvertently enter the human food chain through seafood consumption, leading to potential health risks for individuals who consume these contaminated products over time.

A) Conversely   B) Contrarywise

C) Additionally   D) Oppositely

2. The human microbiome, which comprises trillions of microorganisms that live in and on our bodies, plays a crucial role in maintaining overall health and supporting vital bodily functions. _____, research has shown that disruptions to this delicate ecosystem, whether due to antibiotics or poor diet, have been linked to a variety of diseases, including obesity, diabetes, and even mental health disorders.

A) Inopportunely   B) Elsewise

C) Tactlessly   D) As a matter of fact

3. The rise in global temperatures has led to more frequent and severe heatwaves, wildfires, and hurricanes. These extreme weather events have caused widespread devastation and economic losses. _____, the consequences of climate change are becoming increasingly evident, demanding immediate and decisive action from governments and individuals alike.

A) Indeed   B) Nor

C) Lest   D) Unless

4. Non-governmental organizations (NGOs) often operate in areas where government presence is limited or ineffective, stepping in to provide essential services and support. _____, they play a critical role in global development initiatives by addressing pressing issues like poverty alleviation, education access, and healthcare improvement.

A) Alternatively   B) Therefore

C) To say nothing of   D) In all honesty

5. Social media has intensified political polarization by creating echo chambers where users are exposed primarily to information that reinforces their existing beliefs. _____, it has also facilitated the widespread dissemination of misinformation, which can mislead the public and distort perceptions of reality, further deepening societal divides.

A) As well as this   B) Let alone

C) Furthermore   D) In the first place

6. The history of cryptocurrency and blockchain technology is marked by rapid innovation and development, transforming how we think about money and transactions. _____, it has also been associated with significant concerns over security, potential fraud, and regulatory challenges that authorities are still trying to navigate.

A) Anyways   B) Nor

C) Conceivably   D) On the other hand

C. Punctuation & Boundaries: Select the correct answer from the options provided.

1. Scientists discovered a new species of frog in the Amazon rainforest, a remarkable finding that could help us understand the effects of _____

A) climate change   B) climate change!

C) climate change"   D) climate change.

2. After a long day of classes, homework, and extracurricular _____ students find themselves overwhelmed and exhausted. This fatigue can affect their performance and motivation in the following days.

A) activities, many   B) activities many

C) activities many,   D) activities many;

3. Have you ever wondered why the sky is blue, especially during a clear day when the sunlight seems to make it even _____ This question has fascinated scientists and curious minds alike for centuries.

A) more vibrant!   B) more vibrant-

C) more vibrant,   D) more vibrant?

Test 16

A. Sentence Form and Structure
Select the choice that conforms to the conventions of Standard English.

1. Excerpt from a term paper: *"Every nation goes through significant historical events that shape national identity and future. _____."*

A) The Civil War was, like, a really big deal back in the day

B) The Civil War was super important, trust me

C) You won't believe how brutal the Civil War was

D) The American Civil War was a pivotal and devastating conflict

2. To be concise and complete, the Magna Carta's significance lies in its _____

A) establishment of the principle that everyone, including the king, was subject to the law.

B) role in establishing the rule of law, limiting monarchical power, and laying the foundation for modern governance.

C) groundbreaking document that established the important principle that everyone, including the monarch, was subject to the law.

D) significant because it established for the first time the principle that all people, including the ruler.

3. As artificial intelligence systems become more sophisticated and integrated into society, ethicists grapple with the implications of _____ capabilities in various fields such as healthcare, finance, and law.

A) its decision-make

B) their decision-making

C) our decision-making

D) his decision-make

4. The series of novels _____ readers around the world for its intricate plots and memorable characters, showcasing the author's unique storytelling ability.

A) is loved by   B) are loved by

C) were loved by   D) have loved by

5. During the high-stakes business merger, the complex financial deal _____ by the corporate lawyers and _____ by the regulatory authorities.

A) was negotiated meticulously / was duly approved

B) the lawyers negotiated skillfully / was approved duly

C) negotiated intensively / was approved cautiously

D) was carefully negotiated / the authorities approved diligently

6. The orchestra performed a symphony by a renowned composer, attracting a large crowd to the concert hall. The performance _____ from critics and audiences alike, highlighting the skill of the musicians and the conductor.

A) receive rave reviews

B) receiving rave reviews

C) received rave reviews

D) receives rave reviews

7. The development of the polio vaccine by Jonas Salk was a major medical achievement. With _____, the threat of this debilitating disease was greatly reduced worldwide, saving countless lives and improving public health.

A) they decided to go forward

B) it being inevitable

C) Salk lead

D) the widespread distribution of this life-saving immunization

B. Idioms

Select the correct answer from the options provided.

1. Instead of using a pre-made cake mix, she decided to bake a birthday cake _____, carefully measuring each ingredient and following the recipe to perfection. The result was a delicious masterpiece.

A) in haste

B) on the fly

C) in a pinch

D) from scratch

2. The students _____ as they prepared for the upcoming final exams, determined to achieve their academic goals and secure their futures. The late nights were exhausting but necessary.

A) burned the midnight oil

B) dropped in the bucket

C) played it by ear

D) took a rain check

3. Faced with economic uncertainty, businesses of all sizes are _____, struggling to adapt to the changing market conditions and find new strategies for success. They must collaborate to survive.

A) barking up the wrong tree

B) on different paths

C) in the same boat

D) calling it a day

4. After a long hike, the cold, refreshing drink _____ perfectly, quenching my thirst and invigorating my spirit. It was just what I needed after the strenuous trek.

A) hit the spot

B) fell flat

C) missed the mark

D) made their day

5. Feeling _____ with a persistent cough and runny nose, she decided to stay home from work and focus on recovering. Rest was essential for getting back on her feet.

A) on top of the world

B) under the weather

C) in a funk

D) over the moon

C. Missing Words: Select the correct answer from the options provided.

Climate zones, the Earth's thermal belts, are fundamental determinants of environmental conditions and human lifestyles. The tropical zone, renowned for its year-round warmth and copious precipitation, serves as a cradle for an extraordinary array of (1) _____ (flora, machinery, architecture, species) adapted to flourish in its sweltering embrace. In contrast, the temperate zone experiences a cyclical rhythm of seasons, providing opportunities for diverse agricultural practices while also presenting farmers with the challenges posed by (2) _____ (extreme, mild, stagnant, predictable) weather fluctuations.

At the opposite end of the climatic spectrum lies the polar zone, a realm of icy desolation characterized by scant vegetation and a (3) _____ (fragile, robust, vibrant, dynamic) ecosystem delicately balanced on the precipice of change. A profound comprehension of these climatic divisions is imperative, as they exert a substantial influence on (4) _____ (migration, technology, philosophy, art) patterns, resource accessibility, and the overall strategies employed by humans to adapt to their surroundings.

Test 17

A. Sentence Form and Structure

Select the choice that conforms to the conventions of Standard English.

1. By next year, I _____ marking a significant milestone in my language learning journey. This achievement will not only reflect my dedication and perseverance but also open doors to new opportunities for communication and connection, enriching my understanding of different cultures and perspectives.

A) will have studied English for three years,

B) have studied English for three years,

C) study English for three years,

D) am studying English for three years,

2. The town, once bustling with activity and filled with the sounds of laughter and commerce, _____. The once-vibrant streets, lined with shops and cafes, are now empty, and the echoes of the past—memories of community gatherings and celebrations—are all that remain, haunting the deserted sidewalks.

A) had fall in disrepair after the factories closed

B) falls into disrepair after the factories closed

C) has fallen in disrepair after the factories closed

D) fell into disrepair after the factories closed

3. The Silk Road, a vital trade route connecting East and West, facilitated _____.

A) the exchange of goods, cultures, and ideas

B) the exchanging of goods, cultures, and the spread of ideas.

C) the exchange of goods, the cultures share, and ideas spreading.

D) the goods exchange of sharing, of cultures, and spreading of ideas

4. In the heart of the city, the new library opened last week. It features modern architecture and extensive collections. _____ many residents visited to explore its offerings.

A) The weather was nice,

B) As it was a weekend,

C) It was also crowded

D) They were anxious

5. Neither Freud nor Jung could have predicted how _____, shaping everything from literature to film and altering perceptions of the human psyche. Their ideas continue to resonate in contemporary discussions about mental health and identity.

A) their theories would influence popular culture

B) them theories would influenced popular culture

C) our theories would influenced popular culture

D) its theories would influence popular culture

6. The plays of Henrik Ibsen, often called the *"Father of Realism,"* _____ characters and social issues in 19th-century European society, challenging audiences to confront the realities of their time.

A) portrays complex

B) portray complex

C) is portraying complex

D) have been portraying complex

7. The ancient Egyptians built the pyramids _____, reflecting their beliefs about the afterlife and the significance of burial practices in their culture.

A) for the purpose of serving as tombs for their pharaohs.

B) to be pharaohs tombs for theirs

C) as tombs for their pharaohs

D) The pyramids served as tombs for ancient Egyptian pharaohs.

B. Transitions: Select the correct answer that completes the text with the most logical transition.

1. Sustainable development aims to create a harmonious balance between economic growth and environmental protection, ensuring that both can coexist for future generations. _____, this complex goal requires active cooperation and collaboration among governments, businesses, and communities to create solutions that are equitable and sustainable for all stakeholders involved.

A) Additionally   B) Despite

C) Not to mention this   D) Alternatively

2. Artificial intelligence is increasingly being utilized in the field of education to personalize learning experiences tailored to the unique needs of each student. _____, this advanced technology can assist educators in identifying specific challenges and strengths, enabling them to address students' individual needs more effectively and improve overall learning outcomes.

A) On the other hand   B) Possibly

C) In addition   D) Much less

3. Sharing economy platforms, such as Uber and Airbnb, have fundamentally revolutionized traditional industries by introducing innovative business models that leverage technology and community resources. _____, these changes have also raised important questions about labor rights, worker protections, and regulatory challenges that need to be addressed to ensure fair practices in this new economic landscape.

A) Or   B) Furthermore

C) However   D) If

4. Automation is transforming the labor market by significantly reducing the need for human workers in certain industries, leading to concerns about job displacement and economic inequality. _____, it also has the potential to create new jobs in emerging fields that require different skills, presenting opportunities for workforce retraining and adaptation.

A) Perhaps   B) To say nothing of

C) In its place   D) Besides this

5. Space exploration is not only expensive but also comes with significant risks, including potential loss of equipment and the safety of astronauts. _____, it offers remarkable potential for scientific discovery and technological advancement that can benefit humanity in numerous ways, from satellite communication to advancements in materials science.

A) Nor   B) What is more

C) Maybe   D) To tell the truth

6. The study initially seemed to support the theory that increased carbon emissions were the sole cause of climate change; however, upon closer examination, the researchers discovered that, _____, a combination of deforestation and industrial pollution also played significant roles in accelerating the warming process.

A) to say nothing of   B) actually

C) nor   D) or

C. Punctuation & Boundaries: Select the correct answer from the options provided.

1. What an incredible _____ years of hard work and perseverance, she finally completed her first marathon, something she had dreamed of for years.

A) achievement, after   B) achievement-After

C) achievement/ after   D) achievement! After

2. She had one goal _____ a published author. With dedication and hard work, she believed she could achieve it. Writing was her passion, and she spent countless hours honing her craft, attending workshops, and seeking feedback from peers.

A) in mind: to become   B) in mind to become

C) in mind, to become   D) in mind; to become

3. The weather was perfect for a _____ was shining, and the birds were singing, creating a picturesque scene that invited relaxation and enjoyment.

A) picnic the sun   B) picnic; the sun

C) picnic. the sun   D) picnic: the sun

Test 18

A. Sentence Form and Structure

Select the choice that conforms to the conventions of Standard English.

1. Despite the warnings from local tribes and seasoned explorers, the adventurers _____ unaware of the dangers that awaited them in the shadows. Their determination was unshaken, fueled by dreams of discovery and quest, even as the foliage grew denser and the cacophony of wildlife echoed around them, creating an atmosphere thick with both excitement and trepidation.

A) had ventured into deep the jungle,

B) would be venturing deep into the jungle,

C) venture into deep the jungle,

D) ventured deep into the jungle,

2. The Mayflower Compact was signed by the Pilgrims before _____ in the New World, establishing a governing framework that would guide their new settlement and reflect their commitment to self-governance and community cooperation.

A) its disembarked   B) their disembarked

C) they disembarked   D) we disembarked

3. During the intense soccer match, both teams fought hard for victory. As the clock ticked down and the score was tied at the last minute, the tension in the stadium reached its peak. _____, and the sudden goal changed everything, sending the crowd into a frenzy and dramatically altering the outcome of the game, leaving fans on the edge of their seats.

A) The referee blew the whistle,

B) Everyone was nervous

C) Then one player scored

D) Fans were cheering loudly.

4. George Orwell's novel "*1984*" depicts a dystopian society where the government exercises total control over _____.

A) people's thoughts, actions, and emotions.

B) thoughts and actions, and society be emotional.

C) people's emotional thoughts, responses, and actions

D) thought actions of the people, and emotions.

5. During the conference on climate change, _____, raising concerns among researchers about the potential for catastrophic sea-level rise and the subsequent impact on coastal communities worldwide.

A) The polar ice caps were melting at an alarming rate, the scientists' notes.

B) the scientist noted that the polar ice caps were melting at an alarming rate

C) The scientist, while studying the melting of the polar ice caps noted the effects of climate change.

D) the melting of the polar ice caps studying the effects of climate change, noted by the scientist

6. The astronauts on the International Space Station have been conducting experiments on _____ zero gravity on plant growth, aiming to understand how microgravity influences biological processes and potential future space agriculture.

A) the effects of   B) it's effects for

C) their effects   D) theirs effects in

7. In the heart of the remote jungle, the dedicated team of botanists embarked on an expedition to explore uncharted territory. During their research, a new species of plant _____ by the team, and its unique characteristics _____ in a scientific journal, shedding light on its ecological significance and potential uses in medicine.

A) was discovered coincidentally / were published

B) discovered accidentally / was published

C) had been discovered carefully / were printed

D) were found / circulated

B. Idioms

Select the correct answer from the options provided.

1. The constant ticking of the clock and the looming deadline had him _____, unable to focus on anything else but the impending project submission. The pressure was overwhelming.

A) in hot water

B) under the weather

C) out of the woods

D) on edge

2. The emergency sirens blared through the neighborhood, sending everyone into a panic. However, it turned out to be a _____, and everyone gradually returned to their normal routines, relieved it was just a drill.

A) false alarm

B) close call

C) real scare

D) wake-up call

3. Despite his humble beginnings, he had risen through the ranks of the company to become a _____, commanding respect and influence in the industry. His journey inspired many.

A) black sheep

B) big shot

C) small fry

D) bad-mouth

4. When asked about the complex scientific theory, the professor shrugged and replied, "_____. *That's a question for a physicist.*" His honesty reflected his expertise in other areas.

A) Beats me

B) No clue

C) Fall on our feet

D) Quiet as a cat

5. She was always eager to join in the fun but disappeared as soon as things got difficult, revealing her true colors as a _____, leaving her friends feeling betrayed.

A) loyal companion

B) fair-weather friend

C) steadfast ally

D) supportive mentor

C. Missing Words: Select the correct answer from the options provided.

Democracy, a system of governance rooted in the notion of popular rule, empowers citizens to actively participate in shaping the policies that affect their lives. A cornerstone of this political framework is the (1) _____ (challenge, principle, faction, characteristic) of popular sovereignty, which posits that governmental authority is derived from the explicit consent of the governed. While democracy manifests in diverse forms, including direct and representative models, each carries its own set of (2) _____ (weaknesses, limitations, complex, strengths).

Nonetheless, the democratic ideal is confronted by a myriad of challenges, such as the imperative to conduct free and fair elections and to safeguard the rights of minority groups against the potential (3) _____ (transparency, participation, tyranny, accountability) of the majority. Moreover, the proliferation of misinformation and the deepening of political divisions can erode public confidence in democratic institutions, fostering (4) _____ (apathy, engagement, enthusiasm, stability) among the citizenry and jeopardizing the very foundations of democratic governance.

Test 19

A. Sentence Form and Structure
Select the choice that conforms to the conventions of Standard English.

1. Excerpt from an encyclopedia: *"The Library of Alexandria, founded in the early 3rd century BCE, was one of the largest and most significant libraries of the ancient world. _____, it contained works by the greatest thinkers and writers of antiquity, making it a vital center for knowledge and scholarship in the ancient Mediterranean."*

A) Packed to the brim with old rotten books

B) Housing an extensive collection of scrolls

C) A treasure trove of good stuff

D) Stuffed with all sorts of interesting reads

2. By the time the news _____ too late to act. The once-hopeful plans had crumbled, and the consequences of the delay would reverberate through the days to come, leaving a trail of regret and what-ifs that weighed heavily on the hearts of those involved. Friends and colleagues exchanged worried glances, knowing they had missed their chance to make a difference.

A) will spread, it is already

B) spreads, it was already

C) had spread, it was already

D) is spreading, it had already been

3. The Serengeti ecosystem, renowned for its breathtaking landscapes and diverse wildlife, features the incredible spectacle of the annual animal migration. With _____ migration, it showcases one of nature's most spectacular phenomena, drawing visitors from around the world who come to witness this remarkable event.

A) their annual wilderbeast

B) them annual wildebeest

C) our annual wilderbeast

D) its annual wildebeest

4. The collection of rare stamps, which includes pieces from various historical periods and countries, _____ in the museum. This exquisite collection not only highlights the artistry of philately but also serves as a testament to the rich history captured in each stamp.

A) are displaying   B) were displaying

C) is displayed   D) have displayed

5. For the prestigious literary awards, the winning novel _____ by the acclaimed author and _____ by the discerning judges.

A) was masterfully penned / evaluated thoroughly

B) passionately was penned / critically assessed

C) the author wrote masterfully / was judged meticulously

D) were brilliantly written / the judges reviewed carefully

6. The renowned chef recently opened a new restaurant in the heart of the city, offering a unique dining experience with a focus on locally sourced ingredients. Since its opening, the restaurant _____ from critics and patrons alike.

A) receives rave reviews

B) receive rave reviews

C) has received rave reviews

D) is receiving rave reviews

7. The environmental activist campaigned tirelessly to raise awareness about pollution in the oceans, working diligently to inform the public and influence policymakers. Her efforts _____ regulations on waste disposal, ultimately contributing to a healthier marine ecosystem.

A) lead to stricter

B) leads to stricter

C) leading to stricter

D) led to stricter

B. Transitions: Select the correct answer that completes the text with the most logical transition.

1. The rapid pace of technological advancement has led to significant improvements in healthcare, with breakthroughs in areas such as genomics and artificial intelligence. _____, these innovations have the potential to revolutionize disease prevention, diagnosis, and treatment, ultimately leading to a healthier global population.

A) Nor   B) Firstly

C) In the first place   D) What is more

2. Transhumanism advocates for the use of technology to enhance human capabilities, such as cognitive function, physical strength, and even lifespan. _____, this movement raises profound ethical questions about what it truly means to be human and the implications of altering our biological nature through technological intervention.

A) However   B) To say nothing of

C) Before   D) What if

3. Genetic engineering in humans holds the potential to eliminate certain genetic disorders, potentially leading to healthier lives for future generations. _____, it also raises significant ethical concerns about eugenics, the potential for inequality, and the moral implications of "designing" humans, which can lead to unforeseen societal consequences.

A) Essentially   B) Luckily

C) However   D) In point of fact

4. Big data has revolutionized many industries by enabling organizations to make more informed, data-driven decisions that enhance efficiency and customer satisfaction. _____, it has also raised significant concerns about privacy and security, as the vast amounts of personal data collected can be misused or inadequately protected.

A) On the other hand   B) Really

C) Categorically   D) Exceedingly

5. Cyber warfare represents a growing threat to national security, as state-sponsored attacks on critical infrastructure can disrupt services and compromise sensitive information. _____, governments are increasingly investing heavily in cybersecurity measures to protect their assets and maintain public trust in digital systems.

A) Thoroughly   B) Further

C) Scarcely   D) By a whisker

6. Understanding consumer behavior is crucial for businesses to succeed in today's competitive marketplace, as it allows them to tailor their products and marketing strategies effectively. _____, psychological factors, such as perception, motivation, and emotions, play a significant role in influencing purchasing decisions and shaping consumer preferences.

A) Easily   B) Almost not

C) Only just   D) Actually

C. Punctuation & Boundaries: Select the correct answer from the options provided.

1. "The only limit to our realization of tomorrow will be our doubts _____ Franklin D. Roosevelt, during a speech that aimed to inspire a nation facing economic challenges.

A) of today," said   B) of today, said

C) of today", said   D) of today. Said

2. I _____ already July! The year has flown by so quickly, filled with events, plans, and unexpected surprises.

A) cant believe its   B) can't believe it's

C) cant believe it's   D) can't believe its

3. My sister is a _____ student and a _____ employee, balancing her studies with her responsibilities at work. This dual commitment requires excellent time management skills and determination, as she strives to excel in both areas while maintaining a healthy social life.

A) parttime/ full time   B) part time / fulltime

C) part-time/ full-time   D) part,time / full,time

Test 20

A. Sentence Form and Structure
Select the choice that conforms to the conventions of Standard English.

1. As the storm clouds _____, rolling in with a menacing heaviness, the sailors prepared for rough seas. The sky darkened ominously, casting shadows over the deck, and the air grew thick with the scent of rain and the tension of an impending tempest, while the crew exchanged anxious glances, bracing themselves for the chaos that was about to unfold.

A) gather in the horizon

B) gathered on the horizon

C) are gathering on the horizon

D) had gathered in the horizon

2. My parents were strict about curfew during my teenage years, believing that staying out late could lead to poor decisions and safety concerns. As a result, they _____ when I was in high school, ensuring I adhered to their rules and values.

A) never let me stay out past midnight

B) have never let me stay out past midnight

C) never out lets me stay past midnight

D) had never lets me out stay past midnight

3. The novelist was renowned for her intricate plots and well-developed characters, captivating readers with her storytelling prowess. Her latest book was eagerly anticipated by fans who had followed her work for years. She _____ dedicating countless hours to perfecting each detail and ensuring that her characters resonated deeply with the audience.

A) spend two year writing this novel

B) spends two year writing this novel

C) spent two years writing this novel,

D) spending two years writing this novel,

4. The protagonist's inner turmoil _____ by the author through a series of vivid flashbacks, and the reader's emotions _____ by the author's skillful writing.

A) was explored skillfully / were manipulated

B) explored skillfully / influenced

C) had carefully been explored / were swayed

D) is explored by / was affected

5. The decision of whether to pursue a career in research or industry, which can significantly impact your future, _____, as it ultimately depends on your personal interests and long-term goals.

A) is entirely up to you   B) is entirely up to yours

C) is entirely up to us   D) is entirely up to them

6. In order to succeed in today's political landscape, a political party must appeal to a diverse electorate, encompassing a wide range of backgrounds and perspectives. Consequently, _____ the needs of various constituents, ensuring that different voices are heard and represented in the political process.

A) his platforms often reflect

B) her platforms often reflect

C) their platforms often reflect

D) whose platforms often reflect

7. Charles Darwin is a key figure in the history of science, known for his work on biological diversity. He _____

A) first proposed the theory of evolution by natural selection in *On the Origin of Species.* Book.

B) proposed the theory of evolution by natural selection in *On the Origin of Species.*

C) was the initial person to propose the theory of evolution by natural selection in *On the Origin of Species...*

D) first proposed the hypothesis, of natural selection, by evolution.

B. Idioms

Select the correct answer from the options provided.

1. His incessant chatter and inability to focus on the topic at hand was _____, making the meeting increasingly unproductive. Team members exchanged frustrated glances, wishing he would stay on track.

A) driving everyone up the wall

B) a breath of fresh air

C) music to the ears

D) a game changer

2. The young writer was _____ as the seasoned editor offered valuable feedback and suggestions to improve her manuscript. She listened intently, eager to absorb every piece of advice to enhance her craft.

A) on the fence

B) in the loop

C) all ears

D) out of touch

3. The company implemented a new performance evaluation system that would affect employees _____, from entry-level positions to executive leadership, aiming for a more equitable and transparent workplace.

A) behind-the-scenes

B) to blow a fuse

C) on the fly

D) across the board

4. After losing the championship match, the athlete felt _____, struggling to find motivation to continue training and doubting whether he could ever compete at that level again. His spirits were low, and he needed time to recover emotionally.

A) just for the record

B) up in arms

C) down in the dumps

D) in a good place

5. The new project manager was sharp, organized, and always _____, ensuring that the team met deadlines and exceeded expectations with remarkable ease. Her proactive approach inspired everyone around her to perform at their best.

A) on the ball

B) off the mark

C) in over their head

D) under the radar

C. Missing Words: Select the correct answer from the options provided.

Victorian poetry serves as a rich tapestry interwoven with the contrasting threads of Romanticism and Realism, offering a profound exploration of the human condition. Romantic poets, responding to the rapid industrialization of the era, sought refuge in the realm of (1) _____ (emotion, logic, structure, conformity), exalting the beauty of nature and the sanctity of individual experience. In stark opposition, Realist poets adopted a more grounded perspective, focusing on (2) _____ (idealism, reality, fantasy, abstraction) and presenting unflinching portrayals of everyday life and societal ills.

This dichotomy is exemplified by the works of poets such as Alfred Lord Tennyson, whose poetry often explores the depths of (3) _____ (simplicity, joy, melancholy, escapism), and Thomas Hardy, whose verses unflinchingly confront the harsh realities of human existence. Moreover, the Victorian era was a crucible of immense social and cultural change, characterized by a complex interplay of (4) _____ (stagnation, progress, optimism, despair). These tumultuous times compelled poets to reassess long-held beliefs and to contemplate the profound impact of societal transformations on personal identity.

Test 21

A. Sentence Form and Structure

Select the choice that conforms to the conventions of Standard English.

1. The Bauhaus movement, a revolutionary force in the early 20th century, significantly influenced modern design and architecture. Through _____, a new approach emphasizing functionality and simplicity emerged, reshaping how designers and architects think about form and purpose.

A) they deemed it appropriate and philosophy

B) it makes sense and philosophy

C) the school's innovative teaching methods and philosophy

D) design was the key and philosophy

2. Excerpt from *Peter Pan* by J.M. Barrie: *"All children, except one, grow up. They soon know that they will grow up, and the way Wendy knew was this. One day when she was two years old, she _____ and she plucked a flower and ran with it to her mother."*

A) played in garden,

B) was playing in a garden,

C) had been played in a garden,

D) play in a garden,

3. When a biologist conducts an experiment, _____ must ensure that all variables are controlled, or _____ results could be skewed. This meticulous attention to detail is crucial, as even the slightest fluctuation can lead to misleading conclusions, ultimately affecting the integrity of the scientific research.

A) they; their

B) he; his

C) one; ones

D) we; our

4. The Apollo program required _____

A) technologically massive funding allocation, and there was political commitment.

B) innovation of technology, massive funding, and committing politically.

C) technological innovation, massive funding allocation, and political commitment.

D) that technology be innovated, massive funding be allocated, and commitment of politics.

5. Excerpt from a novel: *"They had forgotten everything, it seemed, but the fact that he was a gentleman whom they had been accustomed to respect. As they _____ and fear, he rose with an effort and walked unsteadily to his horse."*

A) were look at him with admiration

B) looks at him with admiration

C) had been looked at him with admiration

D) looked at him with admiration

6. Excerpt from a company email, a more formal tone to convey the company's professional image. _____.

A) "Hey, make sure to show up on time for your first day!"

B) "Please arrive promptly at 8:00 a.m. on your first day."

C) "Don't be late, or you'll be in trouble."

D) "Feel free to swing by whenever you're ready to start."

7. The new technology _____ the globe, revolutionizing how businesses operate and interact with consumers. From automation in manufacturing to innovative solutions in healthcare, this shift is not merely an evolution but a complete reimagining of processes and practices.

A. is transforming industries across

B. are transformed industries across

C. has been transformed industries across

D. have been transforming industries across

B. Transitions: Select the correct answer that completes the text with the most logical transition.

1. Media plays a crucial role in shaping public opinion on climate change by disseminating information, highlighting scientific findings, and framing the discourse around environmental issues. _____, it can significantly influence policy decisions and elevate public awareness, prompting action from both individuals and governments to address this pressing global challenge.

A) In fact   B) Except

C) Maybe   D) But

2. Artificial intelligence is increasingly being utilized in the creative industries, ranging from music composition to visual arts, enabling new forms of artistic expression and innovation. _____, this advancement raises important questions about the role of human creativity in the digital age and whether machines can truly replicate or replace the nuanced touch of human artists.

A) On the other hand   B) Regrettably

C) Much less   D) Or

3. Globalization has led to increased cultural exchange and economic integration, facilitating the flow of ideas, goods, and services across borders. _____, it has also resulted in the homogenization of cultures, where local traditions and identities may be overshadowed by dominant global influences, raising concerns about cultural preservation.

A) Perchance   B) Besides this

C) Nor   D) Quite the same

4. The use of animals in scientific research has led to significant medical advancements, contributing to breakthroughs in treatments and therapies that save human lives. _____, it also raises ethical concerns about animal welfare and rights, prompting ongoing debates about the moral implications of such practices and the need for stricter regulations.

A) Tactlessly   B) Possibly

C) To say nothing of   D) Conversely

5. Government intervention is often deemed necessary to address income inequality, ensuring that resources are distributed more equitably within society. _____, there is an ongoing debate over how much involvement is appropriate.

A) Indeed   B) Inappropriately

C) However   D) Actually

6. Magical realism in Latin American literature blends the extraordinary with the ordinary, creating a unique narrative style that captivates readers. _____, this genre allows authors to explore complex social and political issues through fantastical elements, often reflecting the cultural and historical realities of their societies.

A) In contrast   B) It could be

C) Unfortunately   D) For this reason

C. Punctuation & Boundaries: Select the correct answer from the options provided.

1. The Great Wall of China stretches over _____ showcasing incredible engineering and historical significance. It was built over several dynasties, each contributing to its structure, and remains a symbol of Chinese history and culture.

A) 13000 mile   B) 13,000 miles,

C) 13000 miles   D) 13000 miles,

2. The protagonist's journey through the desolate landscape was fraught with peril. The harsh weather conditions, the looming threat of wild animals, and the

uncertainty of finding refuge all tested their _____ their will to survive.

A) limits and: B) limits; and

C) limits and   D) limits...and

3. Have you ever considered what motivates people _____ Many individuals are driven by a desire to make a difference in their communities, contributing their time and skills for a greater cause.

A) to volunteer?   B) to volunteer

C) to volunteer;   D) to volunteer,

Test 22

A. Sentence Form and Structure

Select the choice that conforms to the conventions of Standard English.

1. The Bill of Rights, the first ten amendments to the U.S. Constitution, _____ and protections for American citizens. These amendments not only safeguard individual liberties but also serve as a crucial framework for democracy and justice in the nation.

A) guaranteeing fundamental freedoms

B) guarantees fundamental freedoms

C) is guaranteeing fundamental freedoms

D) have guaranteed fundamental freedom

2. Every student in the Advanced Placement classes is responsible for completing _____ project. This requirement is designed to foster independent thinking and encourage students to engage deeply with their chosen topics.

A) their own research

B) them own research

C) its own research

D) they're own research

3. The documentary about ocean conservation highlighted the importance of protecting marine life. It featured stunning visuals and compelling interviews that brought the issues to life. _____ viewers left feeling inspired to take action.

A) So, it was informative,

B) Many were so skeptical,

C) Some found it boring,

D) As the message was clear,

4. Social stratification is a system in which people are ranked according to their _____.

A) wealth, social status, and powerful positions.

B) wealth and status, and society should be powerful,

C) wealth, status, and power

D) wealth, powerful status, and social positions

5. In his later years, the philosopher _____, drawing from a lifetime of experiences and observations. He offered deep insights into the moral fabric that binds societies together, weaving together threads of compassion, integrity, and responsibility.

A) had reflected on the important of ethical living

B) reflects on the important of ethical living

C) reflected on the importance of ethical living

D) was reflecting on the import of ethical living

6. _____, his eyes gleaming with excitement as he carefully unfurled the fragile artifact. Each symbol, meticulously inscribed, told stories of a civilization's long past, rich with mythology and history.

A) Covered in Egyptologist hieroglyphics the examined the ancient papyrus scroll

B) The Egyptologist examined the ancient papyrus scroll covered in hieroglyphics

C) The ancient papyrus scroll was hieroglyphics, examined by the Egyptologist covered

D) The covered in Egyptologist hieroglyphics examined the ancient papyrus scroll

7. In J.K. Rowling's book series "*Harry Potter*," the intricacies of the magical realm are brought to life with captivating detail and imagination. _____ and wonder, drawing readers into a realm of fantasy that is both enchanting and immersive.

A) Its wizarding world is full of magic

B) It's wizarding world is full of magic

C) Their wizarding world is full of magic

D) Theirs wizarding world is full of magic

B. Idioms

Select the correct answer from the options provided.

1. As the winter chill settled in, the once-bustling outdoor market began to dwindle in activity. Vendors who relied on warm weather for their sales knew that their _____, as the frost would soon blanket the vibrant stalls.

A) they have all the time in the world

B) days were numbered

C) to be a permanent fixture

D) to have a long life

2. The couple decided to _____ for a cross-country adventure, excited to explore national parks and immerse themselves in the rich tapestry of cultures they would encounter along the way.

A) cross a bridge before they came to it

B) jumping judas

C) a litmus test

D) hit the road

3. After a long day of hiking and exploring, she fell into a deep sleep, _____, undisturbed by the sounds of nature around her until the morning sun gently woke her.

A) time out

B) second chance

C) sleeping like a log

D) black and blue

4. When asked about the specifics of the meeting, I couldn't recall the details immediately, but _____, I believe the conference is scheduled for late November. I'll verify that information later.

A) off the top of my head

B) right off the bat

C) in the heat of the moment

D) under lock and key

5. I wish I could join you for dinner tonight, but I'm completely swamped with work. Can I take a _____ and reschedule for next week? I promise I really want to catch up!

A) rain check

B) resting her eyes

C) jersey justice

D) jet-black

C. Missing Words: Select the correct answer from the options provided.

The art of crafting a compelling short story hinges on the skillful orchestration of several essential elements. The (1) _____ (setting, theme, plot, style) serves as the narrative's backbone, propelling the story forward through a carefully sequenced progression of events. To captivate readers and evoke genuine emotional responses, characters must be meticulously developed as (2) _____ (dynamic, static, invisible, superficial) figures capable of growth and change.

The (3) _____ (resolution, conflict, climax, context) within which the story unfolds is established by the setting, which imbues the narrative with a distinct atmosphere and mood. Conflict acts as the story's catalyst, introducing challenges that characters must confront, while the underlying (4) _____ (description, dialogue, structure, theme) imparts the story with its deeper meaning, inviting readers to contemplate universal human experiences.

Test 23

A. Sentence Form and Structure

Select the choice that conforms to the conventions of Standard English.

1. By the time I _____, I will be 25 years old. Completing my studies will mark a significant milestone in my academic journey, as I look forward to applying my knowledge in the real world.

A) will have finished my degree

B) have finished degree

C) finish my degree

D) am finishing degree

2. In the music class, the students learned to play different instruments and honed their skills through regular practice. Emma _____ during the recital, captivating the audience with her performance, her fingers dancing gracefully over the keys as the notes filled the room with emotion.

A) play the piano beautifully

B) playing the beautiful piano

C) played the piano beautifully

D) plays the beautiful piano

3. The complex mathematical equation _____ by the brilliant physicist after months of work, and its solution _____ in a prestigious journal, showcasing the groundbreaking research that could change our understanding of physics.

A) was solved elegantly / was published

B) elegantly solved /were distributed

C) had been solved carefully / is issued

D) is solved by / were circulated

4. The responsibility lies with Mark and _____ the project on time, a task that requires dedication and teamwork. Our collaborative effort will be crucial for meeting the deadline and ensuring the project's success, as every detail matters in this endeavor.

A) them, to complete

B) me, to complete

C) myself, to complete

D) mine, to complete

5. The flock of birds _____, their silhouettes cutting across the fading light of autumn. As the colder months approach, these birds instinctively migrate to warmer climates in search of food and better living conditions, following age-old paths passed down through generations.

A) is heading south for the winter

B) are south headed for the winters

C) has heading south for the winters

D) were south headed for the winter

6. Each species has its own unique adaptations, and _____ survival in their environments. These adaptations enable them to thrive in varying conditions, ensuring their continued existence in the face of challenges, whether it be the harshness of winter or the scarcity of resources.

A) strategies that are crucial for

B) strategized that are crucial for

C) strategy that are crucial for

D) strategic that are crucial for

7. When the clock struck midnight, echoing through the grand halls, _____, her breath quickening with each hurried step. She left behind only a glass slipper, a delicate token of her fleeting visit to the world of royalty. As she dashed down the marble stairs, her heart raced with a mix of exhilaration and fear, knowing the magical spell was about to break, and with it, her chance at a life she had only dared to dream of.

A) Cinderella had fled from the palace

B) Cinderella was fleeing from the palace

C) Cinderella fled from the palace

D) Cinderella flees from the palace

B. Transitions: Select the correct answer that completes the text with the most logical transition.

1. Gabriel Garcia Marquez's "*One Hundred Years of Solitude*" is a quintessential example of magical realism, showcasing a narrative style that intertwines the extraordinary with the ordinary. _____, the novel's blend of the fantastical and the mundane reflects the rich cultural heritage of Latin America, illustrating how history and myth coexist in the region.

A) Above all   B) Nevertheless

C) Indeed   D) While

2. Postcolonialism examines the impact of colonialism on literature and culture, revealing how colonial histories shape contemporary narratives. _____, it challenges traditional narratives and gives voice to previously marginalized perspectives, allowing for a richer understanding of cultural identities.

A) Unfortunately   B) Nevertheless

C) In contrast   D) Thus

3. Intertextuality in modern fiction refers to the way texts reference or draw upon other texts, creating a web of connections that enrich the reading experience. _____, this concept emphasizes the interconnectedness of literary works across time and space, highlighting how authors influence each other.

A) And yet   B) As a result

C) In either event   D) Then

4. Toni Morrison's "*Beloved*" uses elements of intertextuality to engage with African American history and folklore, weaving together various narratives to deepen its impact. _____, the novel challenges readers to confront the legacy of slavery in America, prompting reflection on its enduring effects on society.

A) Although   B) Conversely

C) For this reason   D) Nevertheless

5. The rapid industrialization and coastal development of recent decades have unfortunately led to significant declines in marine biodiversity across many regions, with overfishing, pollution, and habitat destruction taking a heavy toll on vulnerable ecosystems. _____, conservationists and marine biologists remain cautiously optimistic, as innovative fishery management practices, marine protected areas, and environmental restoration efforts have shown promise in certain areas.

A) Inversely   B) Nevertheless

C) What if   D) Maybe

6. The team faced unexpected challenges throughout the project. _____, they were able to successfully deliver the final product on time and within budget, impressing the client with their professionalism and problem-solving abilities.

A) But even so   B) Nonetheless

C) Accordingly   D) If

C. Punctuation & Boundaries: Select the correct answer from the options provided.

1. We just received the exhilarating news that we won _____ All our hard work and late nights of preparation truly paid off, and it feels amazing to see our efforts recognized.

A) the science fair?   B) the science fair!

C) the science fair,   D) the science fair

2. There are several essential skills for success in today's competitive _____ communication, teamwork, and adaptability. Each of these abilities enhances employability and prepares individuals for the diverse challenges they may face.

A) job market: B) job market.

C) job-market   D) job market

3. "*The future belongs to those who believe in the beauty of their* _____ Eleanor Roosevelt, a woman known for her inspiring words and dedication to social justice. Her words encourage us to pursue our aspirations with determination and courage.

A) *dreams*, said   B) *dreams*," said

C) *dreams* said   D) *dreams*" said

Test 24

A. Sentence Form and Structure

Select the choice that conforms to the conventions of Standard English.

1. Excerpt from an academic textbook: *"The Voynich manuscript, a handwritten and illustrated codex from the early 15th century, has confounded scholars for centuries. Its text, written in an unknown script, _____ despite numerous attempts at decipherment. The manuscript's origins, purpose, and meaning remain elusive, inviting both curiosity and frustration among linguists and historians alike."*

A) remains a complete, total head-scratcher

B) continues to baffle experts

C) is kinda still a mystery wrapped in an enigma

D) proves that some old-timer had a wicked sense of humor

2. The novel, which _____ several interconnected families, weaving their stories together with a masterful hand, became an instant bestseller. Its intricate plot, filled with twists and turns, and its richly drawn characters—each with their own dreams and struggles—captivated readers worldwide.

A) traces the lives of

B) had traced the live of

C) was tracing the lives of

D) trace the live of

3. The Göbekli Tepe archaeological site in Turkey has forced historians to reconsider _____ civilization and religious practices. This groundbreaking site, dating back to the Pre-Pottery Neolithic period, challenges previously held notions about the social and religious structures of ancient peoples.

A) its understand of early human

B) their understanding of early human

C) our understanding of early human

D) his understand of early human

4. The species found in the tropical rainforest, including countless insects, birds, and mammals, _____ with thousands of plants and animals coexisting in a complex and delicate ecosystem. This remarkable biodiversity plays a crucial role in maintaining ecological balance and supporting life on Earth.

A) is incredible diverse,

B) are incredibly diverse,

C) has incredibly diverse,

D) was incredible diverse,

5. My sister and _____ a surprise party for our parents' anniversary. This celebration is meant to honor their many years of love and partnership, and we want to make it truly special for them. We've been coordinating with family and friends to ensure everything is a delightful surprise.

A) us are planning   B) I are planning

C) myself are planning   D) mine are planning

6. The themes of love and loss _____ by the poet through a series of powerful sonnets, and the reader's heart _____ by the poet's words.

A) were explored deeply / was touched

B) is explored deeply / moved

C) carefully had been explored / is impressed

D) were explored by / could be affected

7. The chef was famous for his unique culinary creations. He enjoyed experimenting with different flavors and ingredients, often pushing the boundaries of traditional cuisine. For the dessert, he _____ with exotic spices, resulting in a dish that tantalized the taste buds and left diners craving more.

A) combine chocolate   B) combining chocolate

C) combines chocolate D) combined chocolate

B. Idioms

Select the correct answer from the options provided.

1. The usually energetic and enthusiastic team lead seemed uncharacteristically withdrawn and distracted during the weekly meeting, appearing a bit _____, which prompted the concerned manager to discreetly check in with them privately after the session, hoping to understand the underlying issue and provide any necessary support or guidance to help them regain their typical focus and positive demeanor.

A) out of sorts

B) in a jam

C) jumped the gun

D) under the weather

2. The constant criticism and negativity from her boss were really _____ and making her dread going to work each day. Day after day, her boss's relentless criticism and negativity took a toll on her.

A) off the mark

B) chasing the wrong lead

C) eating at her

D) in the dark

3. The detective was _____, when she was focusing on the suspect who had a solid alibi, while the real culprit remained in the shadows, evading capture and continuing their crime spree. Despite her best efforts, the detective was misguided.

A) getting under her skin

B) weighing her down

C) biting at her heels

D) barking up the wrong tree

4. She _____ when she found out her flight had been canceled, completely derailing her meticulously planned vacation and leaving her feeling frustrated and overwhelmed. The news of her canceled flight hit her hard. Her meticulously planned vacation was now in disarray, and frustration overwhelmed her.

A) ran the race

B) leaped ahead

C) became bent out of shape

D) dashed forward

5. Taking on the entire project alone seemed like a good idea at first, but he quickly realized he was _____ and needed to delegate tasks to his team to avoid falling behind.

A) bent on doing

B) in over his head

C) gift of the gab

D) afraid of his own shadow

C. Missing Words: Select the correct answer from the options provided.

Social psychology delves into the intricate interplay between individuals and their social environments, exploring phenomena such as conformity and obedience. Conformity is the inclination of individuals to align their thoughts, feelings, and behaviors with those of a (1) _____ (stranger, leader, minority, group) to foster a sense of belonging. Conversely, obedience entails compliance with the directives of an authority figure, often leading individuals to act in opposition to their personal (2) _____ (interests, beliefs, preferences, instincts).

Group dynamics exert a profound influence on these behaviors, as interpersonal interactions and relationships within a group can significantly impact collective decision-making and (3) _____ (cohesion, isolation, conflict, detachment). A comprehensive understanding of these concepts is essential for unraveling the complex interplay between societal pressures and individual actions, as well as for recognizing the potential for (4) _____ (disruption, creativity, solidarity, dissent) within various social contexts.

Test 25

A. Sentence Form and Structure
Select the choice that conforms to the conventions of Standard English.

1. She felt a surge of confidence as she raised her hand, certain that she _____. The years of studying and countless hours spent poring over textbooks had prepared her for this moment, and the knowledge swirled in her mind like a well-rehearsed melody.

A) knew the answer

B) know answer

C) have known the answers

D) had known answers

2. The law of conservation of energy, which states that energy cannot be created or destroyed, _____. It is essential for understanding how systems operate in both theoretical and practical applications of physics. This principle also underpins a wide range of scientific fields, illustrating the interconnectedness of various physical phenomena.

A) is fundamental to it seems like

B) is fundamental to the study of physics

C) is fundamental to energy conserve

D) is fundamental to scientific understand

3. An artist prepared meticulously for the exhibition. _____.

A) Painted with vibrant colors the artist, displayed her latest work in, the gallery.

B) She displayed her latest work in the gallery, which was painted with vibrant colors.

C) The latest work was displayed by her in the gallery painted with vibrant colors.

D) Painted with vibrant colors the display of her in the gallery was the latest work.

4. The Cold War was characterized by _____

A) ideological conflict, proxy wars, and there was an arms race.

B) ideology that conflicted, wars were fought by proxies, and arms were raced to be built.

C) conflicting ideologies, wars fought by proxies, and racing to build arms.

D) ideological conflict, proxy wars, and an arms race.

5. In the culinary competition, the chefs showcased their skills with creative dishes. The judges tasted each creation with great anticipation, their palates eager to experience the unique flavors and presentations. _____ the atmosphere was filled with excitement.

A) As the stakes were high,

B) Many were nervous,

C) Everyone was silent,

D) The kitchen was chaotic,

6. Each of the major economic theories has _____ explanation for market behavior and cycles. These models provide frameworks for understanding the complexities of economic interactions, influencing everything from policy decisions to individual financial strategies.

A) their own   B) they're own

C) his or her own   D) its own

7. A variety of factors, including genetics, environment, and lifestyle, _____ overall health and well-being. Each of these elements plays a significant role, interconnecting in ways that influence a person's physical and mental health outcomes.

A) contribute to an individual's

B) contributes to an individuals

C) is contributing to an individual's

D) are contributing to an individuals

B. Transitions: Select the correct answer that completes the text with the most logical transition.

1. Stephen Hawking's "*A Brief History of Time*" introduces readers to complex concepts in cosmology, making intricate ideas accessible to a general audience. _____, it has become one of the most popular science books ever published, inspiring countless readers to explore the mysteries of the universe.

A) Perhaps

B) Tentatively

C) In contrast

D) As a result

2. Le Chatelier's Principle explains how chemical systems respond to changes in concentration, temperature, or pressure, providing a foundational understanding of chemical equilibrium. _____, it helps chemists predict the direction of chemical reactions under varying conditions, enhancing their ability to manipulate reactions in practical applications.

A) Consequently

B) In contrast

C) Nevertheless

D) Even less

3. The small business owner carefully reviewed the financial projections for the upcoming fiscal year, considering anticipated changes in market conditions, production costs, and customer demand; _____, they decided to adopt a more conservative growth strategy, focusing on streamlining operations, diversifying their product offerings, and strengthening relationships with key suppliers.

A) for that reason

B) possibly

C) in either case

D) whichever happens

4. Conflict theory in sociology focuses on the struggle for power and resources between different social groups, highlighting the dynamics of competition and inequality. _____, it offers a critical perspective on social inequality and injustice, encouraging deeper analysis of societal structures.

A) Possibly

B) And yet

C) Despite

D) And so

5. Jared Diamond's "*Guns, Germs, and Steel*" explores the factors that contributed to the unequal distribution of wealth and power across different societies, investigating historical, environmental, and geographical influences. _____, it challenges the idea that these disparities are the result of inherent differences among people, promoting a more nuanced understanding of human history.

A) In either case

B) Additionally

C) On the off chance

D) Even less

6. The concept of global citizenship emphasizes the responsibility of individuals to contribute to the well-being of the international community, fostering a sense of shared duty and ethical engagement. _____, it encourages a sense of interconnectedness and shared humanity, prompting individuals to think beyond national boundaries.

A) But even so

B) Probably

C) Furthermore

D) Nonetheless

C. Punctuation & Boundaries: Select the correct answer from the options provided.

1. _____ Symphony, completed when he was almost entirely deaf, is considered one of the greatest musical works ever composed. This remarkable piece not only showcases his genius but also serves as a testament to the power of creativity.

A) Beethovens Ninth

B) Beethovens' Ninth

C) Beethoven Ninth

D) Beethoven's Ninth

2. The aroma of freshly baked cookies from the _____ through the English hallway during lunchtime, was a daily temptation for many students.

A) cafeteria wafting

B) cafeteria, wafting

C) cafeteria wafting,

D) cafeteria; wafting

3. The self-made entrepreneur was a true _____ story, illustrating the extraordinary journey of someone who overcame significant obstacles to achieve success.

A) rags-to-riches

B) rags to riches

C) ragstoriches

D) rags to riches,

Test 26

A. Sentence Form and Structure

Select the choice that conforms to the conventions of Standard English.

1. The Hubble Space Telescope, launched in 1990, has provided stunning images of the universe, capturing breathtaking views of distant galaxies, nebulae, and other celestial phenomena. The telescope, _____, has significantly advanced our understanding of space, allowing astronomers to explore the cosmos with unprecedented clarity and detail.

A) which orbits Earth and captures detailed photographs and stuff

B) whose technology has revolutionized astronomy

C) a cool gadget and instrument that

D) designed to observe distant galaxy star

2. The works of Jane Austen, including *"Pride and Prejudice"* and *"Emma,"* _____ in 19th-century England. Through her sharp wit and keen observations, Austen critiques the societal pressures placed on women and the class distinctions that defined her era.

A) explore social norms and expectations

B) explores social norm and expectations

C) is exploring social norm and expectations

D) have been exploring social norms and expectations

3. After the meeting _____, the members were more determined than ever to achieve their goals. The discussions had ignited a renewed sense of purpose among them.

A) had conclude   B) concluded

C) is concluding   D) concludes

4. After years of hard work, Emily finally launched her own business. She had faced many challenges along the way, including financial setbacks and moments of self-doubt. _____ her determination never wavered, showcasing her resilience and commitment to her entrepreneurial dream.

A) Even though times were tough,

B) Perhaps, she was nervous,

C) But the market was competitive,

D) Many rightfully doubted her and

5. F. Scott Fitzgerald's novel *"The Great Gatsby"* explores the themes of _____. Through its intricate characters and vivid settings, the narrative delves into the complexities of human relationships and the elusive nature of the American Dream, revealing the stark contrasts between wealth and happiness.

A) love, greed and the dream, of America.

B) love greed, and society should be dreamy

C) love, greedy characters, and the American Dream!

D) love, greed, and the American Dream

6. _____ This transformative period marked a significant shift in production methods, leading to the emergence of factories and unprecedented economic growth across Europe and North America.

A) Rapidly new machines were invented, the economy began to grow.

B) The economy began to grow, new machines were invented rapidly.

C) New machines were invented during the Industrial Revolution, and the economy began to grow rapidly.

D) The economy began to shrink rapidly during the Industrial Revolution, new machines were invented.

7. The ancient Greeks believed that _____ and goddesses lived on Mount Olympus. This belief was central to their mythology, influencing their culture, religion, and understanding of the world around them.

A) their gods   B) there god's

C) they're gods   D) theirs god's

B. Idioms

Select the correct answer from the options provided.

1. The customer service representative had _____ with the manager regarding the recent policy change that had caused significant inconvenience to customers, leaving many frustrated and dissatisfied.

A) no love lost

B) a bone to pick

C) bite the bullet

D) a boon in disguise

2. As the fragile antique vase was carefully removed from the box, the movers reminded each other, "_____!" They understood the importance of handling the item with great care to avoid any damage.

A) easy does it

B) Jack Frost

C) Yeoman's service

D) snake in the grass

3. Having worked at the company for over a decade, she truly _____ and could efficiently handle even the most complex tasks without needing any guidance from others.

A) stirred hornets' nest

B) jumped on the bandwagon

C) was in the dark

D) knew the ropes

4. When the consultant analyzed the situation, they _____, pinpointing the root cause of the problem and offering a clear and concise solution that everyone could understand.

A) found the calling

B) missed the mark

C) hit the nail on the head

D) got it twisted

5. The jealous coworker constantly _____ their colleagues behind their backs, spreading rumors and negativity that created a toxic work environment for everyone involved.

A) changed horses in midstream

B) bad-mouthed

C) hit the bull's-eye

D) threaded their way out of

C. Missing Words: Select the correct answer from the options provided.

Population distribution, the spatial pattern of human settlement across the Earth's surface, is a complex phenomenon shaped by a confluence of environmental, economic, and sociopolitical factors. A pivotal influence on population density is (1) _____ (climate, elevation, culture, technology), with regions endowed with favorable climatic conditions often experiencing higher population concentrations. Moreover, the availability of (2) _____ (obstacles, resources, restrictions, traditions) serves as a powerful catalyst for population growth, as areas rich in natural and human-made resources tend to attract a larger workforce.

The inexorable march of urbanization has dramatically altered population distribution, as individuals increasingly migrate to (3) _____ (rural, peripheral, urban, isolated) centers in pursuit of economic opportunities, educational institutions, and a wider range of amenities. Lastly, the dynamics of social and political conditions, including the presence or absence of (4) _____ (isolation, harmony, conflict, distance), significantly shape population patterns, as periods of unrest can lead to population displacement, while stable environments tend to foster population growth.

Test 27

A. Sentence Form and Structure

Select the choice that conforms to the conventions of Standard English.

1. My grandmother used to _____ when I was a child. They were not just treats; but a cherished tradition that filled our home with warmth and the enticing aroma of baking sweets. Each year, I eagerly anticipated her special recipes, which brought the family together during the holiday season.

A) make delicious cookies every Christmas

B) made delicious cookie's each Christmas

C) has made delicious cookies each Christmas

D) had made delicious cookies' every Christmas

2. The historic treaty _____ by the world leaders after years of negotiation, and its terms _____ in a formal ceremony. This landmark agreement not only aimed to bring peace but also established frameworks for future cooperation among nations, marking a pivotal moment in diplomatic history.

A) had been signed carefully / were announced

B) ceremoniously signed was / announced

C) was signed ceremoniously / were announced

D) were signed by / would be announced

3. The prize was awarded to Jane and _____ outstanding research. Our work not only contributed to the field but also inspired others to explore new avenues of inquiry, demonstrating the impact of our dedication and intellectual rigor.

A) me for our   B) me for us

C) myself for our   D) mine for us

4. In 1848, gold was discovered at Sutter's Mill in California, sparking the Gold Rush. Thousands of prospectors, _____ in search of fortune. This massive influx of hopeful individuals transformed the landscape and culture of the region, as dreams of wealth and prosperity drove many to brave the arduous journey.

A) known as "forty-niners," traveled westward

B) who were hoping to strike it rich! traveled westwards

C) seeking wealth and adventure: traveled west ward

D) whose dreams of gold. traveled westward

5. The lecture _____. It provided a comprehensive overview of key events, influential figures, and the socio-political dynamics that shaped one of history's most powerful civilizations.

A) covers the rise and fell of the Roman Empire

B) covered the rise and fall of the Roman Empire

C) covering the rise and fall of the Roman Empire

D) cover the rise and fell of the Roman Empire

6. Excerpt from *Fahrenheit 451* by Ray Bradbury: *"It was a pleasure to burn. It was a special pleasure to see things eaten, to see things blackened and changed. With the brass nozzle in his fists, with this great python spitting its venomous kerosene upon the world, the blood pounded in his head, and his hands _____ smile come again on his face."*

A) grips the immense snake and felt the old

B) had gripped the immense snake and felt the old

C) gripped the immense snake and felt the old

D) grip the immense snake and felt the old

7. To put it simply, social inequality _____.

A) refers to the unequal distribution of resources and opportunities among different kinds of groups.

B) is the disparity in wealth as well as the difference in opportunities among social classes

C) describes situations where resources might not be shared equally among people.

D) exists when resources and opportunities are distributed unevenly

B. Transitions: Select the correct answer that completes the text with the most logical transition.

1. Power dynamics in international relations significantly influence the behavior of nations, shaping alliances and conflicts on a global scale. _____, understanding these dynamics is crucial for effective diplomacy and conflict resolution, as it enables leaders to navigate complex geopolitical landscapes.

A) Conversely   B) Then

C) Hence   D) Even more

2. In his seminal work, Yuval Noah Harari's *"Sapiens: A Brief History of Humankind"* meticulously examines the evolution of human societies from the Stone Age to the present day. _____, it explores how various aspects of human culture, economy, and political structures have collectively shaped the modern world we live in today.

A) In addition   B) While

C) Nevertheless   D) As a result

3. Behavioral economics investigates how psychological factors and cognitive biases influence economic decision-making processes. _____, it provides valuable insights into the reasons why individuals sometimes make seemingly irrational financial choices, challenging traditional economic theories based on rational behavior.

A) Then again   B) But

C) And so   D) For this reason

4. The novel's exploration of existential themes profoundly challenges traditional notions of meaning and purpose in life. _____, it provides a thought-provoking examination of the human condition that resonates with readers from diverse backgrounds, encouraging introspection and philosophical inquiry.

A) Thus   B) In this case

C) However   D) Conversely

5. Recent research highlights the critical role of renewable energy sources in combating climate change and ensuring sustainable development. _____, the evidence underscores the urgent need for immediate and sustained action from both policymakers and the global public to mitigate environmental impacts and transition to a greener economy.

A) In sum   B) For starters

C) On the other hand   D) Despite

6. The marketing team, tasked with developing a new brand strategy, conducted extensive consumer research and analyzed industry trends; _____, they proposed a comprehensive plan that would modernize the company's visual identity, enhance digital outreach, and forge stronger emotional connections with the target audience, all to drive increased brand loyalty and market share.

A) feasibly   B) meanwhile

C) perhaps   D) along these lines

C. Punctuation & Boundaries: Select the correct answer from the options provided.

1. The new _____ on the company website) outlines the rules for employee conduct. This document aims to ensure a professional work environment and sets clear expectations for behavior.

A) policy (available   B) policy [available

C) policy available   D) "policy available

2. The author emphasized three critical themes in her _____ struggle for identity, the impact of cultural heritage, and the quest for personal freedom.

A) novel the,   B) novel the

C) novel, the   D) novel: the

3. In her keynote speech, the scientist referenced the article _____ and Its Impact on Global Agriculture" to underscore the urgency of adopting sustainable practices and solutions.

A) Climate-Change   B) , Climate Change

C) "Climate Change   D) Climate Change

Test 28

A. Sentence Form and Structure

Select the choice that conforms to the conventions of Standard English.

1. Excerpt from a formal and historical article: *"The Terracotta Army, a remarkable collection of terracotta sculptures depicting the armies of Qin Shi Huang, the first Emperor of China, _____ to protect him in his afterlife. This monumental creation, discovered in 1974 near the city of Xi'an, serves not only as a testament to the artistic and engineering prowess of ancient China but also reflects the emperor's beliefs about the afterlife and the importance of having a protective force in the next world."*

A) was buried with the big boss

B) got stuck underground for like ages

C) was interred with the emperor

D) ended up as really really old statues

2. In 2008, housing prices in the United States reached unsustainable levels, leading to a dramatic collapse and a global financial crisis. Many analysts _____ was fueled by risky lending practices and speculative investments. The rapid increase in home values was driven by a combination of factors, and a belief that housing prices would continue to rise indefinitely, ultimately resulting in severe economic repercussions.

A) asserted that this housing bubble

B) asserts that housing bubble

C) were asserting that this housing bubble

D) are asserting that housing bubble

3. To be concise and complete, the Doppler effect _____.

A) is the change in frequency or wavelength of a wave for an observer moving relative to its source

B) alters wave frequency/wavelength for moving observers,

C) is a phenomenon that occurs when there is a change in the frequency or wavelength of a wave as perceived by an observer who is moving relative to the source of the wave

D) is experienced by an observer moving relative to the source of a wave, characterized by a change in the perceived frequency or wavelength of the wave.

4. The Polynesian voyagers, renowned for _____, traversed vast stretches of the Pacific Ocean long before European explorers. This allowed them to discover and settle numerous islands across the Pacific.

A) its celestial navigation skill

B) their celestial navigation skills

C) his celestial navigation skills

D) her celestial navigation skill

5. Excerpt from *East of Eden* by John Steinbeck: *"For many years, he had been at the mercy of the wind. It _____ the plains, whistling through the gaps in the walls, tugging at his clothes and thoughts alike."*

A) had blew across   B) has blown across

C) was blowing across   D) blowing across

6. It was _____ suggested the new marketing strategy. Her innovative approach aimed to increase brand visibility and engagement, reflecting a deep understanding of market trends and consumer behavior.

A) her, whose   B) herself, who

C) hers, who   D) she, who

7. The rescue team was praised for their swift response during the natural disaster. They worked tirelessly to help those in need. The team _____ during the operation.

A) save many lives   B) saves many lives

C) saved many lives   D) saving many lives

B. Idioms

Select the correct answer from the options provided.

1. After a long and tumultuous relationship, the news of their breakup hit her hard, leaving her feeling lost and alone. She had invested so much emotionally in the relationship, and now she faced an uncertain future. The breakup truly _____, shattering her hopes for their future together.

A) crushed her spirit

B) put a smile on her face

C) brightened up her day

D) lifted her mood

2. The recently renovated kitchen was a sight to behold. With everything sparkling clean and shining like new, it was clear that a great deal of effort had gone into the updates. Everyone who entered remarked how it was _____, reflecting the meticulous work of the renovation team.

A) messy and disorganized

B) clean as a whistle

C) a work in progress

D) cluttered with boxes

3. Throughout their many years together, the couple faced numerous challenges, including financial difficulties and personal loss. Yet, their relationship only grew stronger as they supported one another. They truly stood by each other _____, proving their deep commitment to one another despite the odds.

A) during sunny days

B) for a short time

C) in moments of joy only

D) through thick and thin

4. In the recent board meeting, the CEO emphasized the importance of profitability. She stated that the _____ is that we need to increase sales by 20% to meet our quarterly targets, which is crucial for ensuring the company's growth and stability moving forward.

A) side issue

B) bottom line

C) unimportant trivia

D) secondary consideration

5. After an exhausting day filled with meetings and deadlines, she felt completely drained. Recognizing that she needed rest, she decided to call it a night and _____, knowing that a good night's sleep would help her recharge for the challenges awaiting her the next day.

A) stay awake

B) dwell on her worries

C) catch some Z's

D) rush into work

C. Missing Words: Select the correct answer from the options provided.

A constitution is a foundational legal document that delineates the framework of a government, enshrining the fundamental rights and responsibilities of its citizenry. At its core lies the establishment of (1) _____ (ideas, amendments, levies, imposts) that safeguard individual liberties, such as freedom of expression and religion. These inalienable rights are indispensable for fostering a (2) _____ (democratic, authoritarian, chaotic, uniform) polity where citizens can freely participate in the political process and hold their government accountable.

Beyond delineating individual rights, constitutions also impose civic obligations upon citizens, emphasizing the imperative of (3) _____ (participation, remoteness, triviality, unconcern) in democratic processes, including voting and jury service. To ensure its enduring relevance, a constitution must possess the flexibility to accommodate societal evolution, allowing for (4) _____ (rigor, torpor, adaptation, turmoil) in response to emerging challenges and aspirations.

Test 29

A. Sentence Form and Structure

Select the choice that conforms to the conventions of Standard English.

1. The Golden Age of Islam, spanning from the 8th to the 14th century, _____ advancements in mathematics, astronomy, medicine, and philosophy. During this remarkable period, scholars from diverse backgrounds collaborated to preserve and enhance knowledge, leading to groundbreaking discoveries. Innovations such as algebra, the astrolabe, and advancements in medical practices emerged.

A) produce significant

B) produces significant

C) produced significant

D) have produced significant

2. The League of Nations, _____, failed to prevent World War II. Established after World War I to promote peace and cooperation among nations, the League aimed to resolve disputes through diplomacy rather than conflict.

A) despite its noble intentions

B) despite their noble intention

C) despite his noble intentions

D) despite her noble intention

3. In 1999, during the dot-com boom, technology stocks surged to unprecedented heights, only to plummet shortly afterward. _____ was characterized by investor speculation in internet companies without regard to their profitability.

A) Experts believe that this bubble

B) Experts believed that this bubble

C) Expert have believed that this bubble

D) Expert believing that this bubble

4. The ancient manuscript, which _____, was finally found in a dusty attic. The fragile pages held secrets that had been long forgotten, waiting to be brought to light.

A) was lying undiscovered for centuries

B) has lain undiscovered for centuries

C) had lain undiscovered for centuries

D) lay undiscovered for centuries

5. The Indian Rebellion of 1857 was sparked by a combination of factors, including _____. This uprising, often referred to as the Sepoy Mutiny, was not merely a revolt against British rule but rather a culmination of deep-seated grievances felt by various segments of Indian society.

A) political, economic, and social grievances

B) political and economic, and society should be social

C) political, economic grievances, and social unrest;

D) politics, economical, and grievances of the society!

6. The engineer, who _____ the beginning, was praised for his innovative solutions and unwavering dedication. His leadership was crucial to the initiative's success.

A) is overseeing the project from

B) has oversee the project from

C) oversees the project from

D) had overseen the project from

7. Acids and bases can neutralize each other through a chemical reaction. During _____ produces water and salt, demonstrating the balance of pH levels. Understanding this process is fundamental in chemistry, as it illustrates how different substances can interact to form new compounds while maintaining equilibrium in their environments.

A) it, their interaction

B) this process, their interaction

C) their, this interaction

D) the solution, this interaction

B. Transitions: Select the correct answer that completes the text with the most logical transition.

1. The digital divide refers to the significant gap between individuals and communities who have access to digital technologies and those who do not, often resulting in disparities in education, employment, and social engagement. _____, addressing this divide is crucial for ensuring equal opportunities in the digital age, as it empowers all individuals to participate fully in society.

A) Generally   B) To resume

C) By the way   D) Thus

2. Opportunity cost is the economic concept that defines the value of the next best alternative that must be sacrificed when a choice is made. _____, it serves as a fundamental principle in economics, helping individuals and businesses make rational decisions by evaluating the potential benefits of different options.

A) By the way   B) In short

C) As previously stated   D) To get back to the point

3. "*The Black Swan*" by Nassim Nicholas Taleb dives into the profound impact of highly improbable and unpredictable events on our lives and decision-making processes. _____, it challenges our traditional understanding of risk and uncertainty, prompting us to rethink how we approach forecasting and planning in an unpredictable world.

A) Before I forget   B) To resume

C) In sum   D) Maybe

4. The principle of separation of powers is a cornerstone of democratic governance, ensuring that no single branch of government becomes too powerful or authoritarian. _____, this system of checks and balances not only maintains democratic stability but also upholds accountability among elected officials.

A) Indeed   B) Perhaps

C) In contrast   D) But

5. Romantic poets of the 19th century sought to express the sublime beauty of nature as a profound response to the rapid industrialization of their time. _____, their work often reflected a deep reverence for the natural world, contrasting sharply with the mechanization and urbanization that characterized their era.

A) Moreover   B) In the interim

C) Conversely   D) Meanwhile

6. Jane Austen's "*Pride and Prejudice*" is not only a novel of manners that intricately explores themes of love and social status but also delves into the complexities of personal development and moral growth. _____, it reveals how characters navigate societal expectations while pursuing their own happiness and identity.

A) To resume   B) Moreover

C) Anyhow   D) Perhaps

C. Punctuation & Boundaries: Select the correct answer from the options provided.

1. The upcoming career fair aimed to connect students with potential _____ from various industries who would be available to answer questions and discuss career opportunities.

A) employer's   B) employers'

C) employers's   D) employers

2. So, what makes a great _____ communication, empathy, and vision are often cited as key qualities. Leadership can take many forms, depending on the context, and each leader may exhibit different strengths that contribute to their effectiveness.

A) leader? Effective   B) leader-effective

C) leader: effective   D) leader, effective

3. The recipe called for _____ of milk, ensuring that the dish would have the right texture and flavor. This precise measurement is crucial in baking, where ingredients need to be balanced for the best results.

A) 3;4 cup   B) 3/4 cup

C) 3,4 cup   D) 3-4 cup

Test 30

A. Sentence Form and Structure

Select the choice that conforms to the conventions of Standard English.

1. By the time the summer arrives, I _____, hoping to finally pass on this attempt after learning from my previous mistakes and gaining more confidence behind the wheel.

A) will have taken my driving test twice

B) have taken my driving test twice

C) take my driving test twice

D) am taking my driving test twice

2. Researchers _____ significant progress in understanding genetic mutations over the past decade. This area of study is crucial for advancements in medicine and biotechnology, as it helps identify the underlying causes of various genetic disorders.

A) might had made   B) have made

C) make   D) making

3. The new software application, which _____ during several intense sessions, _____ by the development team to ensure that every feature functioned seamlessly and met the high standards expected by users in today's fast-paced digital environment.

A) brainstormed enthusiastically / coded efficiently

B) was brainstormed innovatively / was coded meticulously

C) the team brainstormed innovatively / was expertly coded

D) was collaboratively brainstorm / the developers coded precisely

4. The team of engineers demonstrated _____ during the conference, showcasing innovative designs and cutting-edge technology that not only addressed current industry challenges but also paved the way for future advancements in sustainability and efficiency.

A) them solution to complex problems

B) they solution to complex problems

C) their solutions to complex problems

D) those solutions to complex problems

5. The characters in the novel, each with their own unique backgrounds and motivations, _____, contributing significantly to the overarching themes of love and betrayal. The author skillfully develops each character, allowing readers to connect with their personal journeys and understand their complex relationships.

A) is vividly portrayed   B) are vividly portrayed

C) has vivid portrayed   D) was vivid portrayed

6. The Odyssey is an ancient Greek epic poem attributed to Homer. It follows the adventures of Odysseus, _____ encounters various challenges on his journey home from the Trojan War.

A) who, face a lot of trials

B) a kind of legendary figure who

C) whose went on journey

D) the Greek hero, who

7. Excerpt from an academic paper: *"The Indus Valley Civilization, one of the world's earliest urban cultures, flourished in the northwestern regions of South Asia from 3300 to 1300 BCE. Archaeological evidence suggests that _____ sophisticated urban planning, advanced drainage systems, and standardized weights and measures."*

A) these ancient folks were pretty ahead of their time, boasting

B) this remarkable civilization demonstrated

C) these smart cookies managed to create

D) the Indus Valley people surprisingly had

B. Idioms

Select the correct answer from the options provided.

1. Despite the urgent need for a decision on the new policy, the committee members continued to _____, debating minor details and postponing meetings, which ultimately frustrated the stakeholders who were eager to see progress and implementation.

A) jump at the chance

B) take the initiative

C) hit the ground running

D) drag their feet

2. Faced with mounting financial difficulties, the family made the tough decision to _____ and sell their beloved vacation home, knowing it was the best option for their future. The emotional attachment to the property made the choice even more challenging.

A) take the easy way out

B) play it safe

C) stick to their guns

D) bite the bullet

3. Losing weight is _____, as it requires dedication, discipline, and consistent effort over time to achieve lasting results. Despite the allure of quick fixes and fad diets, sustainable weight loss demands commitment and lifestyle changes.

A) easier said than done

B) a piece of cake

C) a walk in the park

D) a simple task

4. The seasoned actor delivered a flawless performance, having memorized his lines _____, proving his professionalism and dedication to the craft. His commitment to mastering the script contributed to the authenticity of his portrayal.

A) by chance

B) by heart

C) on a whim

D) in a hurry

5. The outdated technology was deemed _____ in today's competitive market, as it lacked the features necessary to attract modern consumers. Despite its historical significance, practical utility outweighed sentimentality.

A) not worth a hill of beans

B) a valuable asset

C) a hidden gem

D) a cutting-edge solution

C. Missing Words: Select the correct answer from the options provided.

Modernist literature emerged as a radical departure from traditional literary conventions, reflecting the fractured and disorienting nature of the modern world. A hallmark of modernist texts is their embrace of (1) _____ (fragmentation, consistency, simplicity, predictability) in narrative structure, challenging the linear progression and causal relationships characteristic of earlier literary forms. This stylistic innovation invites readers into a realm of (2) _____ (ambiguity, clarity, monotony, certainty), demanding active engagement and interpretation rather than passive consumption.

Modernist authors were pioneers in their experimentation with (3) _____ (imagery, themes, language, characters), subverting conventional syntax, grammar, and punctuation to create new modes of expression. The judicious employment of (4) _____ (uniformity, directness, symbolism predictability) enabled modernist writers to construct intricate layers of meaning, encouraging readers to delve beneath the surface and explore the complexities of the human psyche and the modern condition.

Test 31

A. Sentence Form and Structure

Select the choice that conforms to the conventions of Standard English.

1. Excerpt from a respectful and slightly reverential editorial piece: *"The Taj Mahal, an ivory-white marble mausoleum in Agra, India, was commissioned in 1632 by the Mughal emperor Shah Jahan to house the tomb of his favorite wife, Mumtaz Mahal. This architectural masterpiece _____ art and design, showcasing an exquisite blend of Persian, Indian, and Islamic influences."*

A) is when you come right down to it, the bests expression of love

B) stands as a testament to the emperor's cool taste

C) represents the pinnacle of Indo-Islamic

D) is hands down the most beautiful building

2. Excerpt from a reflective travelogue: *"Machu Picchu, the ancient Incan city set high in the Andes Mountains of Peru, remains one of the most remarkable archaeological sites. This breathtaking location _____, the sophistication of Incan engineering and their harmonious relationship with the natural landscape."*

A) highlights the important of tourism in Peru

B) represents a lost civilization's architectural prowess

C) is often cite as a wonders of the modern world

D) showcase the beauty of the Andean region

3. The ideas presented by various philosophers throughout history, such as Plato and Kant, _____ modern thought and ethical discussions in contemporary society. Their insights have shaped our understanding of morality, justice, and the human condition, prompting ongoing debates that resonate with current philosophical inquiries.

A) is influencing   B) were influential

C) was influenced   D) have been influencing

4. When discussing ethical theories, it is important to analyze how _____ apply to modern dilemmas. Understanding the foundations of these theories provides valuable insights into navigating complex moral landscapes and making informed decisions in an increasingly interconnected world.

A) one's principals   B) one's principles

C) the principals   D) them principles

5. Complex equations _____ problems. These equations often arise in various fields such as engineering, physics, and economics, where they play a critical role in modeling complex systems and providing solutions to practical challenges.

A) use by students to solve real-world

B) are used by students to solve real-world

C) used by students' to solve real-world

D) is using by students to solve real-world

6. Sociologists _____ in the past to analyze their impact on society. By studying movements such as civil rights, feminism, and environmental activism, researchers gain insights into the dynamics of social change and the factors that contribute to the success or failure of these movements.

A) have studied various social movements

B) have been studying, various social movement

C) could study various social movements

D) studying various social movements

7. As part of their annual charity event, the local community center hosts a variety of activities to raise funds for different causes. For the past five years, they _____ that attracts participants of all ages, fostering a sense of community and encouraging healthy lifestyles among residents.

A) organize a charity run

B) have organized a charity run

C) had organize a charity run

D) are organizing a charity run

B. Transitions: Select the correct answer that completes the text with the most logical transition.

1. Big data refers to the vast amounts of data generated by digital technologies, which can be analyzed to reveal patterns, trends, and associations. _____, it enables new insights and innovations across various fields, from healthcare to marketing, ultimately transforming how decisions are made and strategies are developed.

A) By the way   B) A propos

C) So   D) But

2. "*Sapiens: A Brief History of Humankind*" by Yuval Noah Harari meticulously traces the evolution of human societies from prehistoric times to the present. _____, it explores how cognitive, agricultural, and scientific revolutions have fundamentally shaped our world and influenced the trajectory of human development.

A) Anyhow   B) Parenthetically

C) In short   D) To resume

3. Constructivism in international relations emphasizes the profound role of ideas, beliefs, and identities in shaping state behavior and interactions. _____, it challenges the notion that international relations are solely driven by material factors such as military power and economic resources, highlighting the importance of social constructs.

A) In a nutshell   B) To get back to the point

C) Longwindedly   D) By the way

4. In classic prose, the sentence structure is often carefully balanced to reflect the formality of the genre. _____, it may adopt a more fluid style to match the narrative tone and thematic elements, allowing for a more engaging reading experience that captures the reader's attention.

A) Or else   B) Furthermore

C) Tactlessly   D) Temporarily

5. The Amazon River is the largest by volume in the world, serving as a crucial waterway for both ecological and human activity. _____, it supports an incredible diversity of wildlife, making it a focal point for conservation efforts and a vital resource for local communities.

A) Maybe   B) Perchance

C) It could be   D) Likewise

6. The team struggled to meet the project deadline, _____ did they manage to stay within the budget, ultimately leading to a series of setbacks that required extensive revisions and additional resources to complete the task successfully.

A) nor   B) however

C) conversely   D) yet

C. Punctuation & Boundaries: Select the correct answer from the options provided.

1. The weather was perfect for a _____ sun was shining brightly in the clear blue sky, and the birds were singing cheerfully from the branches of the trees. Families gathered in the park to enjoy the day together, spreading blankets on the grass and sharing laughter and stories.

A) picnic, the   B) picnic; the

C) picnic-the   D) picnic the

2. During the intense trial, the witness confidently stated, "*The suspect _____ who was wearing a red jacket _____ fled the scene quickly.*" This testimony was crucial, as it provided a clear description of the individual involved, allowing the jury to visualize the events as they unfolded.

A) [...]   B) . .

C) ;...;   D) "..."

3. It's important to remember that everyone has a unique perspective shaped by their individual experiences and backgrounds. _____ experiences shape their views, and this diversity of thought is what makes discussions so rich and engaging.

A) People's   B) Peoples"

C) People   D) Peoples

Test 32

A. Sentence Form and Structure
Select the choice that conforms to the conventions of Standard English.

1. By the time the concert started, the audience _____ seats for nearly an hour. Anticipation filled the air as attendees mingled and shared their excitement about the performance.

A) has been sitting in theirs

B) have been sitting in theirs

C) will have been sitting in their

D) had been sitting in their

2 The discovery of X-rays by Wilhelm Röntgen revolutionized medical diagnosis. _____, doctors gained a non-invasive way to examine internal body structures, enhancing their ability to diagnose and treat a variety of conditions with unprecedented accuracy.

A) After they checked

B) After it came about

C) After this breakthrough in 1895

D) After Röntgen was ended

3. When Galileo was conducting astronomical observations, _____.

A) he observed the moons of Jupiter using his improved telescope

B) using improved telescope the moons, of Jupiter were observed by him.

C) the Jupiter moons were observed using his improved telescope by him

D) the moons of Jupiter-observed by him using his telescope improved

4. The city, once known for its vibrant cultural scene filled with art galleries, theaters, and lively festivals, _____ over the past few decades. The changes, both physical and social, have reshaped its identity entirely, as new developments rise alongside historic landmarks, and the community adapts to the evolving landscape, blending tradition with modernity.

A) underwent a dramatical transformation

B) has undergone a dramatic transformation

C) is undergone in a dramatic transformation

D) had undergo a dramatic transformation

5. *Pride and Prejudice*, a novel by Jane Austen, explores themes of love and social class in 19th-century England. The story centers on Elizabeth Bennet, _____, and independent spirit set her apart from other characters. Her journey through societal expectations and personal growth reveals the complexities of human relationships and the challenges women faced during that era.

A) a young woman whose sharp wit

B) who had intelligence and was sharply wit

C) who is ill-known, for her sharp wit

D) a person whom using sharp wit

6. The captain ordered that the ship _____ was loaded, knowing that time was of the essence. The crew, disciplined and efficient, moved with purpose, securing the last of the supplies and preparing to set sail without delay, their eyes fixed on the horizon, eager for the adventure that awaited them.

A) departs immediate after the cargo

B) depart immediately after the cargo

C) departed immediately after the cargo

D) will depart immediate after the cargo

7. The United Nations Security Council must reach a consensus before _____ action. This requirement ensures that all member states agree on significant decisions concerning international peace and security.

A) it can take

B) they can takes

C) he can takes

D) she can take

B. Idioms

Select the correct answer from the options provided.

1. After the product failed to meet customer expectations, the development team had to _____ and rethink their strategy to better align with market demands. The setback required a fresh approach and careful consideration of their next steps.

A) call it a day

B) stick to their plan

C) put the finishing touches

D) go back to the drawing board

2. The designer handbag cost a _____, but it was a coveted item among fashion enthusiasts who valued exclusivity. Its price tag reflected its quality, craftsmanship, and status symbol.

A) pretty penny

B) petty cash

C) couple of dollars

D) mere trifle

3. Before returning to work, the employees decided to _____ at the nearby food court, eager to refuel for the busy afternoon ahead. Taking a short break allowed them to recharge and maintain productivity.

A) go on a diet

B) work through lunch

C) cook a meal

D) grab a bite to eat

4. With exams just around the corner, it was _____ for the students, who spent long hours studying and preparing to achieve their desired grades. The pressure intensified as they aimed for success.

A) crunch time

B) a time for relaxation

C) a leisurely period

D) a moment of calm

5. When the customer service representative was unable to resolve the issue, the customer _____, raised their voice and demanded to speak to a manager immediately. Frustration and impatience fueled their reaction.

A) keep their cool

B) flew off the handle

C) took a deep breath

D) held their temper

C. Missing Words: Select the correct answer from the options provided.

Poetry, a captivating art form, employs a diverse array of linguistic devices to conjure evocative images and emotions within the reader's consciousness. Central to poetic expression is (1) _____ (simplicity, structure, imagery, rhythm), a technique that harnesses vivid language to create sensory experiences and stimulate the imagination. By forging unexpected connections between disparate concepts, poets can imbue their work with profound depth and resonance using (2) _____ (humor, statement, truth, metaphor), a figure of speech that equates one thing to another, often revealing hidden similarities.

Another essential poetic tool is (3) _____ (analogy, simile, cliché, uniformity), which draws explicit comparisons between unlike entities, typically employing the words "like" or "as" to illuminate descriptions. Moreover, poets animate the inanimate through (4) _____ (detachment, abstraction, personification, monotony), a device that bestows human qualities upon nonhuman objects and forces, thereby fostering a sense of intimacy and connection with the natural world.

Test 33

A. Sentence Form and Structure

Select the choice that conforms to the conventions of Standard English.

1. Neither the economic downturn nor the political instability _____ the country's overall progress. In recent years, the nation has faced numerous challenges, including fluctuating markets and shifting governmental policies.

A) has significantly impacted

B) have significantly impacted

C) is having significantly impact

D) are having significantly impact

2. The *Harry Potter* series, written by J.K. Rowling, has captivated millions of readers worldwide. The protagonist, Harry Potter, _____ embarks on a journey to defeat the dark wizard Voldemort. This journey not only involves magical battles but also deep friendships, personal growth, and the struggle against evil, making the narrative rich and multifaceted.

A) a naive young wizard with a lightning-shaped scar on that adorns his forehead

B) whose bravery and determination:

C) who discovers his magical heritage,

D) the central player who

3. The Fibonacci sequence has fascinated mathematicians since _____ in the 13th century. This intriguing mathematical pattern, where each number is the sum of the two preceding ones, appears in various natural phenomena, from the arrangement of leaves on a stem to the spirals of shells. Its connection to the golden ratio has further captivated artists and scientists alike.

A) its discovery   B) their discover

C) his discover   D) her discovery

4. In the world of technology, innovations emerge at a rapid pace. Companies compete to create the next groundbreaking device, pushing the boundaries of what is possible. _____ consumers often feel overwhelmed by choices, as the market becomes flooded with various products, each promising to enhance their daily lives.

A) Yet they are loyal,

B) They are too much excited,

C) The market is beyond saturated,

D) As a result,

5. William Golding's novel *Lord of the Flies* explores the effects of isolation on _____. Set against the backdrop of a deserted island, the narrative digs into the psychological and social consequences of being cut off from civilization.

A) individuals, groups, and society.

B) individuals and groups, and society should be whole.

C) individual groups, and the whole of society.

D) individuals, groups, and the society as a whole.

6. _____. The research process involved meticulous planning and execution, ensuring that every variable was accounted for.

A) Carefully the data was collected, the scientist analyzed it,

B) The scientist analyzed it carefully, the data was collected.

C) The scientist analyzed it carefully while conducting the experiment, and the data was collected.

D) The data was collected while experimenting, and the scientist analyzed it carefully

7. The environmental science club organized a cleanup event at the local park, inviting students and community members alike to participate. The success of the event was largely due to _____ in removing litter, planting trees, and educating attendees about environmental conservation.

A) us dedicated effort   B) our dedicated efforts

C) dedicate effort   D) dedicate ourselves effort

B. Transitions: Select the correct answer that completes the text with the most logical transition.

1. The concept of economic inequality highlights the significant disparities in wealth and income distribution within societies. _____ it is often linked to social unrest and political instability, as marginalized groups may feel disenfranchised and seek change through protests or other means.

A) If so   B) So much so that

C) Unfortunately   D) Awkwardly

2. "*Capital in the Twenty-First Century*" by Thomas Piketty provides a thorough examination of the dynamics of wealth concentration in modern economies. _____, it has sparked intense debates on how to effectively address economic inequality and promote a more equitable distribution of resources.

A) Likewise   B) For this reason

C) Next   D) Initially

3. The festival attracted visitors from all over the region, showcasing local art, music, and cuisine, _____ that it not only boosted the economy significantly but also fostered a sense of community pride and cultural appreciation among residents and attendees alike.

A) to such a degree   B) with this intention

C) afterward   D) initially

4. The exploration of Mars has revealed the planet's potential for past microbial life, prompting scientists to reconsider the possibility of life beyond Earth. _____, these findings have intensified efforts to study Mars more closely for future human colonization and potential resource utilization.

A) Furthermore   B) Let alone

C) Quite the opposite   D) On the contrary

5. The works of William Wordsworth are central to the Romantic literary movement, emphasizing emotion and the beauty of nature as vital elements of human experience. _____, his poetry often captures the profound impact of natural beauty on the human psyche, reflecting deep philosophical insights.

A) In contrast,   B) If

C) Perhaps   D) In fact

6. Few people can fully grasp the complexities of string theory in physics, _____ explain its implications for our understanding of the universe. This highlights the intricate nature of theoretical physics, which often challenges even the most educated minds.

A) moreover   B) also

C) let alone   D) as well

C. Punctuation & Boundaries: Select the correct answer from the options provided.

1. The critic wrote, "*The novel's plot is engaging, and the characters are well-developed _____, the pacing in the middle sags somewhat.*"

A) -However   B) ; however

C) ... However   D) "however

2. In the world of technology, innovations such as artificial intelligence, virtual _____ blockchain are transforming industries at an unprecedented pace. Each advancement brings both challenges and opportunities that require careful consideration. Staying informed about these developments is essential for success in today's rapidly evolving landscape.

A) reality and   B) reality; and

C) reality. And   D) reality, and

3. Why do we celebrate _____ These vibrant events foster community spirit and preserve traditions, allowing people to share their heritage with others. They serve as a reminder of our shared history and the importance of diversity in our society.

A) cultural festivals   B) cultural festivals"

C) cultural festivals?   D) cultural festivals:

Test 34

A. Sentence Form and Structure

Select the choice that conforms to the conventions of Standard English.

1. If I _____ work schedule and numerous commitments, I would enthusiastically attend the concert with you, relishing the opportunity to enjoy the music and share the experience.

A) weren't so busy with my demanding

B) am not so busy with my demand

C) haven't been so busy with my demanding

D) wasn't so busy with my demand

2. The philosopher Confucius, a central figure in Chinese thought, emphasized ethics, morality, and social order. His teachings, _____, have had a profound influence on Chinese society and culture. Confucius's philosophies have shaped numerous aspects of daily life, governance, and interpersonal relationships, establishing a framework that continues to resonate in contemporary society.

A) that sometimes focus on relationships harmony

B) whose impact extends beyond China

C) being a guide for personal behavior and societal

D) which emphasized elders respects

3. Students _____ in the lab to explore chemical reactions since the semester began.

A) conducted various experiment

B) conducts various experiment

C) have conducted various experiments

D) conducting various experiment

4. During the sold-out rock concert at the massive stadium, the band's latest hit song _____ by the energetic musicians and _____ by the ecstatic audience.

A) be passionately performed / sung enthusiastically along

B) was brilliantly performed / is sung loudly along

C) the electrifyingly band performed / fervently, it was sung along

D) was passionately performed / sung enthusiastically along

5. In the literature seminar, the professor asked _____ of the classic novel. This collaborative approach fostered everyone's participation in thought-provoking discussions about literature.

A) I to analyze the central themes

B) me to analyze the central themes

C) my to analyzes the central themes

D) mine to analyzed the central themes

6. The theories of cognitive development proposed by psychologists like Piaget and Vygotsky _____ individuals learn and grow throughout different life stages.

A) is still offer valuable insights into how

B) has been still offer valuable insights into how

C) are still offering valuable insights into how

D) was still offering valuable insights into how

7. In the intricately woven tapestry of the novel, the author meticulously develops a multifaceted knight. _____, desires, and motivations propel the plot forward. These motivations guide the character's choices, shape his relationships, and ultimately determine the course of events.

A) His inner struggles

B) Their inner struggle

C) Her inner struggles

D) Its inner struggle

B. Idioms

Select the correct answer from the options provided.

1. After a grueling twelve-hour shift at the bustling hospital, where life-and-death decisions were made, the utterly exhausted surgeon decided to _____ and head home to rest, as he felt a strong urge to recharge and gather his strength for the demanding challenges that awaited him the following day.

A) push through

B) call it a day

C) pull an all-nighter

D) go the extra mile

2. Instead of providing a direct and candid response to the sensitive and probing question posed by the journalist, the seasoned politician resorted to _____, skillfully offering vague statements that did little to clarify the complex situation for the public or the press.

A) hitting the nail on the head

B) getting to the point

C) lay it on the line

D) beating around the bush

3. The unexpected and thrilling news of their team's stunning victory in the championship match sent the enthusiastic fans into a frenzy, as they _____, jumping and cheering in jubilant celebration, filled with elation and pride for their beloved team's achievement.

A) went bananas

B) held their horses

C) took it in stride

D) be level-headed

4. Solving the simple algebraic equation, which baffled many of his peers, was _____ for the gifted mathematician, who effortlessly arrived at the correct solution within mere seconds, displaying an impressive level of skill and intuition that left others in awe.

A) harder than rocket science

B) uphill battle

C) tough as nails

D) as easy as pie

5. The elderly gentleman, with a twinkle in his eye and a smile that hinted at fond memories, confessed that he _____ watching the squirrels scamper energetically up and down the old oak tree in his backyard, finding joy in their playful antics and lively spirit.

A) was indifferent to it

B) was afraid of it

C) got a kick out of

D) beat his brain out

C. Missing Words: Select the correct answer from the options provided.

Memory is a complex process that involves several key stages, allowing us to retain and recall information. The first step is (1) _____ (retrieval, recovery, encoding, forgetting), where information is transformed into a format that can be processed by the brain. Once encoded, this information moves into (2) _____ (storage, analysis, perception, distraction), where it is maintained over time for future use.

The ability to access this stored information is known as (3) _____ (retrieval, deciding, decay, interference), which can be influenced by various factors such as emotional state and context. However, not all information is retained indefinitely; (4) _____ (remembering, recalling, forgetting, recognizing) can occur, leading to the loss of memories that may once have seemed significant. Understanding these processes helps illuminate how we learn and interact with the world around us.

Test 35

A. Sentence Form and Structure

Select the choice that conforms to the conventions of Standard English.

1. The researchers, _____ to the success of the project and significantly advanced our understanding of the subject, were praised for their invaluable contributions to the field of study.

A) who data is crucial

B) whom data is crucial

C) whose data was crucial

D) which data was crucial

2. It was a bright cold day in April, and the clocks were striking thirteen. Winston _____ his breast in an effort to escape the vile wind that whipped through the streets, carrying with it the chill of uncertainty and the weight of a world on the brink. He pulled his coat tighter around him, bracing against the gusts that seemed to carry whispers of a distant past.

A) had sunk his chin nuzzled into

B) sunk his chin nuzzle in

C) sinks his chin nuzzles into

D) was sink his chin nuzzled in

3. Excerpt from a scholarly and informative text: "The Code of Hammurabi, a Babylonian legal text composed around 1750 BCE, _____ principle of justice that formed the foundation of legal systems in ancient Mesopotamia and influenced subsequent laws throughout history."

A) laid down the law and showed everyone who's boss in

B) established the cool "an eye for an eye" motto

C) codified the lex talionis as a fundamental

D) was all about getting even and making sure people behaved

4. The DNA molecule, often referred to as the blueprint of life, carries genetic information that determines the characteristics of an organism. This complex structure,

_____, has been the subject of intensive scientific research and holds the promise of profound implications for the future of medicine and genetics.

A) that is composed of nucleotides...

B) whose discovery was a breakthrough

C) being the genetic foundation,

D) which has revolutionize medicine

5. The Pythagorean theorem, a fundamental principle in geometry that has been used by mathematicians for centuries, _____ between the sides of a right triangle. it serves as a crucial tool in various fields, including architecture, physics, and computer science.

A) state the relationship s

B) states the relationship

C) is stating the relationships

D) have stated the relationship

6. Every one of the Nobel laureates, recognized for their exceptional achievements and groundbreaking research, has made _____, showcasing the diversity of their work and its impact on society.

A) significant contributions in their field

B) significant contribution in its field

C) significant contributions in his field

D) significant contribution in they're field

7. While exploring the ancient ruins, the archaeologists uncovered numerous artifacts from a lost civilization. Each discovery revealed new insights into their culture and way of life. _____ the team was excited about their findings, knowing they could reshape historical understanding.

A) Yet, they were not cautious,

B) Everyone was cold,

C) Although the work was tedious,

D) They have been working hard

B. Transitions: Select the correct answer that completes the text with the most logical transition.

1. "*The Lean Startup*" by Eric Ries presents a comprehensive methodology for developing businesses and products in an uncertain environment. _____, it emphasizes rapid iteration and validated learning, encouraging entrepreneurs to test their ideas quickly and adjust based on feedback.

A) By the way   B) To get back to the point

C) As previously stated   D) In sum

2. The committee gathered all relevant data and consulted experts in the field to ensure they made the most informed decisions, and _____, they devised a comprehensive plan aimed at improving community engagement and addressing the concerns raised during the previous meetings.

A) incidentally   B) perhaps

C) with this intention   D) before

3. Malcolm Gladwell's "*The Tipping Point*" examines how small changes can lead to significant societal shifts, exploring the dynamics of influence and change. _____, it explores the factors that contribute to sudden and dramatic changes in behavior and trends, illustrating how minor adjustments can have major effects.

A) Then   B) By the way

C) Consequently   D) In particular

4. Classical mechanics can describe many physical phenomena with great accuracy, particularly at larger scales. _____, quantum mechanics provides a more comprehensive framework for understanding particles at the atomic and subatomic levels, addressing phenomena that classical physics cannot explain.

A) Alternatively   B) Now

C) At the moment   D) So

5. The impact of colonialism on indigenous cultures is profound and far-reaching, affecting social structures and cultural practices. _____, the economic and political consequences continue to shape contemporary global relations, influencing discussions on reparations and cultural preservation.

A) On top of that   B) Conceivably

C) Into the bargain   D) Possibly

6. The northern lights are a spectacular natural phenomenon caused by solar wind interacting with the Earth's magnetic field, creating breathtaking displays in the night sky. _____, their colors and patterns can vary significantly depending on solar activity and atmospheric conditions, making each appearance unique.

A) With fright   B) What is more

C) Doubtfully   D) Uncertainly

C. Punctuation & Boundaries: Select the correct answer from the options provided.

1. I can't believe how beautiful the flowers are in _____ colors are so vibrant and refreshing, creating a stunning display that brightens every garden. Nature truly has a way of lifting our spirits and brightening our days, reminding us of the beauty that surrounds us.

A) springtime! The   B) springtime the

C) springtime" The   D) springtime; the

2. The recipe requires the following _____, sugar, eggs, and vanilla extract. Make sure to follow the instructions carefully, as each step is crucial for achieving the perfect texture and flavor. Baking can be both an art and a science, where precision is key to delicious results.

A) ingredients-flour   B) ingredients flour

C) ingredients, flour   D) ingredients: flour

3. When he exclaimed, _____ to start my new job!" I could see his excitement radiating from him. It was a significant milestone in his career, marking a new beginning filled with possibilities.

A) I can't wait   B) "I can't wait

C) I can't wait,   D) "I cant wait

Test 36

A. Sentence Form and Structure

Select the choice that conforms to the conventions of Standard English.

1. Pierre Bourdieu's concept of cultural capital refers to the idea that _____ in various social contexts. This intricate framework suggests that knowledge, education, and even tastes in art and cuisine serve not merely as personal preferences but as tools for navigating social hierarchies.

A) economic, social, and cultural resources can be used to gain advantage

B) economic and social, and society should be cultural.

C) economic, social resources, and cultural advantage.

D) socio-economic cultural advantages can be gained

2. Excerpt from *Rebecca* by Daphne du Maurier: *"Last night I dreamt I _____. It seemed to me I stood by the iron gate leading to the drive, and for a while I could not enter, for the way was barred to me, shrouded in memories of a past that lingered like a haunting melody."*

A) go with Manderley again

B) went to again Manderley

C) had gone to Manderley again

D) was going with again Manderley

3. _____, known as plate tectonics, can cause natural disasters such as earthquakes and volcanic eruptions, which can have significant impacts on the environment and human activities.

A) The movement of Earth lithospheric plates

B) The movement of Earth's lithospheric plates

C) The movement of Earths lithospheric plate

D) The moment of Earth's lithospheric plate

4. My friends and I _____ every summer since we were kids, creating lasting memories and enjoying the sun together year after year.

A) could go to beach

B) goes to beach

C) have gone to the beach

D) went to the beach

5. In the 1980s, New Zealand faced a dramatic increase in property prices, followed by a significant market correction that caught many investors by surprise. Financial historians _____ bubble was driven by deregulation and speculative lending practices that fueled the market's volatility.

A) contends that this property

B) contended that this property

C) were contending that this property

D) has been contended that this property

6. At the prestigious five-star restaurant, the exquisite gourmet meal, known for its innovative flavors and presentation, _____ by the world-renowned chef and _____ by the highly trained waiter, ensuring a memorable dining experience for every guest.

A) masterfully prepared / was serving elegantly done

B) was prepared artfully / served impeccably

C) creatively prepared / is served professionally

D) was prepared skillfully / will be served gracefully

7. The activists worked tirelessly to promote sustainability, raise awareness, and advocate for change in their community. _____ government, highlighting the impact of grassroots movements.

A) Their efforts were recognized by the local

B) Them efforts were recognize by the local

C) They efforts were recognize by the local

D) Those efforts were recognized by the local

B. Idioms

Select the correct answer from the options provided.

1. The dedicated research team worked tirelessly, going _____, often sacrificing their personal time and sleep to meet the stringent deadline for the groundbreaking scientific experiment that could change the course of their field.

A) slowly but surely

B) in fits and starts

C) ninety to nothing

D) at a leisurely pace

2. The notorious thief, known for his clever tactics and quick escapes, was _____ by the vigilant security guard as he attempted to make off with the valuable artwork from the museum, catching him in the act just in time.

A) off the hook

B) whale of a time

C) flew under the radar

D) caught red-handed

3. Determined to overcome her longstanding addiction to sugary snacks, she decided to quit _____. At once, eliminating all processed treats from her diet and wholeheartedly embracing healthier alternatives that would nourish her body.

A. through a gradual process

B. slow and steady

C. weaning off

D. cold turkey

4. While the generous donation was certainly appreciated by the community leaders, it was merely _____ compared to the massive funds required to rebuild the entire community that had been devastated by the recent floods.

A) a significant amount

B) a large contribution

C) a drop in the bucket

D) game-changer

5. Completing the basic programming exercise, which many novices found challenging, was _____ for the experienced software developer, who effortlessly wrote the code, debugged it, and tested the application in a matter of minutes, showcasing his expertise.

A) a snap

B) an impossible feat

C) a herculean task

D) a tough nut to crack

C. Missing Words: Select the correct answer from the options provided.

Natural resources are vital for sustaining life and supporting human activities. They can be categorized into two main types: (1) _____ (finite, artificial, renewable, depleted) resources, which can be replenished naturally over time, and (2) _____ (non-renewable, sustainable, abundant, reusable) resources, which exist in limited quantities and cannot be easily replaced once consumed.

The sustainable management of these resources is crucial for ensuring their availability for future generations. This involves practices such as (3) _____ (exploitation, conservation, neglect, depletion), which aim to protect and preserve natural environments while balancing human needs. Effective conservation strategies include promoting the use of (4) _____ (synthetic, eco-friendly, hazardous, unnecessary) resources, such as solar and wind energy, to reduce dependence on non-renewable sources and mitigate environmental impacts.

Test 37

A. Sentence Form and Structure

Select the choice that conforms to the conventions of Standard English.

1. Excerpt from a concerned and objective passage: *"The Great Barrier Reef, the world's largest coral reef system, _____ marine biodiversity, providing a vital habitat for countless species. However, it faces significant threats from climate change and ocean acidification that jeopardize its future."*

A) is home to a bunch of cool sea creatures and

B) serves as a crucial habitat for an extensive array of

C) is like an underwater city full of fish and

D) has got more sea life than you can shake a stick at and

2. In essence, black holes _____, representing some of the most fascinating and enigmatic phenomena in the universe that challenge our understanding of physics.

A) are regions in space where the gravitational pull is so strong that nothing, not even light, can escape

B) pull everything in, including light!

C) are like very extremely dense areas in space that trap light

D) are areas in space with tons of gravity

3. Marie Curie, who dedicated her life to scientific research and made groundbreaking discoveries in the field of radioactivity, inspired many women in science. Her groundbreaking work earned _____, highlighting her significant contributions to the scientific community.

A) hers two Nobel Prizes

B) she two Nobel Prizes

C) her two Nobel Prizes

D) herself two Nobel Prizes

4. The ideas presented by various philosophers throughout history, such as Plato and Kant _____ modern thought and ethical discussions in contemporary society, shaping our understanding of morality and governance.

A) continues to influence

B) continue to influence

C) continue to influenced

D) continues to influenced

5. In the late 1990s, the Thai baht collapsed, triggering the Asian financial crisis that had far-reaching effects on economies throughout the region. Analysts _____ that this emergency was preceded by a speculative bubble in the region's real estate and stock markets, which ultimately led to a loss of investor confidence.

A) could claim   B) claims

C) were claiming   D) claimed

6. Democracy, a system of government based on the principles of popular sovereignty and the participation of citizens, has been adopted by many nations around the world. This form of governance, _____, is essential for protecting individual rights and promoting social progress.

A) despite the rose of authoritarian regimes

B) being an idea often difficult to achieved in practice

C) which has faced numerous challenges throughout history

D) that was root in the Enlightenment

7. The study of addiction, which explores the neurobiology and psychology of dependence, has significantly enhanced our understanding of substance use disorders. This complex issue, _____, evidenced by extensive research from various fields, including neuroscience and psychology.

A) that was probably developed in the 20th century

B) whose implications are far-reaching

C) being a critic public health concern

D) which explain the mechanisms of withdrawal

B. Transitions: Select the correct answer that completes the text with the most logical transition.

1. The discovery of exoplanets has significantly expanded our understanding of the universe beyond our solar system, revealing the diversity of planetary systems. _____, this advancement has spurred significant interest in the possibility of extraterrestrial life, prompting new research and exploration initiatives.

A) Furthermore   B) However

C) Unless   D) Instead

2. In classical physics, Isaac Newton's laws of motion provided a comprehensive framework for understanding physical phenomena, establishing fundamental principles of motion and force. _____, his work laid the groundwork for the later development of Einstein's theory of relativity, which transformed our perception of time and space.

A) In lieu of   B) Nevertheless

C) Conversely   D) Moreover

3. The study of urban geography has transformed our understanding of cities and the processes of urbanization, challenging traditional views of spatial organization. _____, it highlights the dynamics of urban development and its implications for social and environmental issues.

A) Parenthetically   B) Additionally

C) In contrast   D) Except

4. The principles of classical mechanics apply to many everyday situations and engineering problems, providing reliable solutions and predictions. _____, they form the basis of many technological advancements that have shaped our modern world, influencing everything from transportation to construction.

A) In fact   B) On the contrary

C) Nevertheless   D) Otherwise

5. Few students grasp the complexities of advanced calculus in their early studies, _____ the more abstract concepts of theoretical mathematics, which require a deeper understanding of mathematical principles and logic.

A) with reference to   B) in addition to

C) let alone   D) in spite of

6. The economic benefits of globalization are evident in increased trade and investment, _____, it can lead to significant social and environmental challenges, including inequality and ecological degradation that need to be addressed.

A) however   B) perhaps

C) despite   D) furthermore

C. Punctuation & Boundaries: Select the correct answer from the options provided.

1. According to Patel (2020), *"Climate change discussions have become more prevalent in recent years, highlighting the urgent need for action and awareness _____ However, despite the overwhelming evidence, many people remain skeptical of the data presented"* (p. 15).

A) discussions;   B) discussions'

C) discussions-   D) discussions...

2. The _____ novel is available in hardcover and paperback editions, appealing to readers who prefer different formats. Each edition offers a unique experience, whether it's the durability of the hardcover or the portability of the paperback.

A) bestselling   B) bestselling,

C) best-selling   D) best=selling

3. The CEO's highly anticipated speech touched on the _____ recent achievements, celebrating milestones that inspired the entire team. This moment was particularly significant, as it highlighted the hard work and dedication that have driven their success.

A) companys"   B) company's

C) company   D) companys

Test 38

A. Sentence Form and Structure
Select the choice that conforms to the conventions of Standard English.

1. The human eye, a remarkably intricate organ, enables us to perceive light and create visual images. This sensory organ, _____, is capable of outstanding feats such as color vision, which allows us to distinguish between a vast range of hues, and depth perception.

A) whose function is essential for survival

B) which can consists of several parts

C) be sensitive to light and dark,

D) that can be perhaps affected by various conditions

2. The complex interplay of gravitational forces between celestial bodies, creates a delicate balance within the cosmos. This gravitational relationship, which influences everything from the orbits of planets to the formation of galaxies, _____ structure that allows for the existence of diverse astronomical phenomena.

A) require a harmonious

B) are requiring a harmonious

C) is requiring a harmonious

D) requires a harmonious

3. Excerpt from a persuasive and encouraging email:
"Dear Valued Customer, we appreciate your loyalty and want to share something exciting with you. Our latest product has been designed with your needs in mind, offering innovative features that can enhance your daily experience. _____

A) "You should totally buy our new product, it's the best."

B) Discover how our new product can transform your daily routine!"

C) If you want to be more productive, you better consider our new product."

D) "Our new product is pretty cool, you might like it."

4. In the meantime, someone _____ towards the camp, moving with the quiet precision of a shadow. He was none other than Sherlock Holmes, who had been observing the whole scene from a distance, piecing together clues and unraveling the mystery with his keen intellect, ready to intervene at just the right moment.

A) made his way stealthily

B) makes his way stealth

C) had made his way stealth

D) was making his way stealthily

5. The committee members couldn't reach a consensus on the matter at hand, which caused _____ the decision that many had hoped would provide clarity and direction. This lack of agreement led to further discussions being postponed, creating uncertainty among stakeholders.

A) they to delay   B) them to delay

C) their to delay   D) themselves to delay

6. None of the information presented during the meeting _____ the current investigation, highlighting the need for more comprehensive data to support the ongoing inquiries. This lack of pertinent details has hindered the progress of the case and raised concerns about the validity of the findings.

A) are relevant to   B) is relevant to

C) have relevance with D) were relevance with

7. In her thesis, Jenna argued that childhood experiences shape adult behavior, and _____ supported the hypothesis, providing substantial evidence drawn from various psychological studies. This rigorous research not only enhanced her argument but also contributed to the broader understanding of developmental psychology.

A) their finding   B) whom findings

C) hers finding   D) her findings

B. Idioms

Select the correct answer from the options provided.

1. The impatient student, filled with excitement and anxiety about the upcoming exam, _____ and opened the exam paper before the teacher had given the signal to start, causing a stir among his classmates who were still waiting for instructions.

A) played it safe

B) followed instructions

C) waited patiently

D) jumped the gun

2. The slow and inefficient bureaucracy, notorious for its convoluted processes and endless paperwork, was _____, causing unnecessary delays and frustration for everyone involved in various projects, from employees trying to navigate the system to clients waiting for approvals.

A) a necessary evil

B) a smooth operation

C) a pain in the neck

D) a blessing in disguise

3. After pulling an all-nighter to finish the report, an exhausting feat that required immense concentration and effort, she was absolutely _____ and could barely keep her eyes open, struggling to stay alert during the important morning meeting.

A) raring to go

B) full of energy

C) alive and kicking

D) dog-tired

4. I know the answer to the question, and it's right _____; I just can't quite remember it at the moment, despite having studied the material thoroughly and feeling confident about my knowledge just a few minutes ago.

A) on the tip of my tongue

B) out of sight, out of mind

C) gone with the wind

D) at my fingertips

5. With multiple deadlines approaching rapidly and a growing list of tasks to complete, the project manager was _____ in work, struggling to juggle all the responsibilities while trying to maintain a sense of order and efficiency.

A) up to the neck

B) free as a bird

C) ahead of schedule

D) on top of things

C. Missing Words: Select the correct answer from the options provided.

Political parties play a crucial role in the political landscape of any democracy. Their primary function is to (1) _____ (organize, disrupt, confuse, isolate) political activity by bringing together individuals with similar ideologies and goals. They serve as a bridge between the government and the public, helping to (2) _____ (reject, obscure, diminish, articulate) the interests and concerns of citizens.

Political parties also engage in the process of (3) _____ (withdrawing, disbanding, electioneering, ignoring), campaigning for candidates and seeking to win seats in legislative bodies. The structure of political parties can vary significantly, leading to different (4) _____ (ideologies, frameworks, party systems, strategies) such as single-party, two-party, or multi-party systems, each influencing governance and policymaking in unique ways.

Test 39

A. Sentence Form and Structure

Select the choice that conforms to the conventions of Standard English.

1. Excerpt from *Frankenstein* by Mary Shelley: *"He was soon borne away by the waves and lost in darkness and distance, swallowed by the relentless sea. I _____, heedless of the surf that broke over my feet, feeling the cold saltwater wash around my ankles as I strained to catch a final glimpse, my heart heavy with a sense of desperation and longing."*

A) have fled to the water edge

B) was fleeing to the waters' edge

C) fled to the water's edge

D) had fled to the waters edge

2. Excerpt from a novel: *"We were all silent until he _____, to speak much, but when he did, we knew to listen. His words carried weight, resonating with the unspoken truths that lingered in the air, and each utterance seemed to draw us closer to the depths of his thoughts, inviting us into a realm of profound reflection."*

A) speaks again. It was not its nature to talk

B) had spoken again. It was not his nature to talk

C) spoke again. It was not his nature to talk

D) will speak again. It was not it's nature to talk

3. Geologists were eager to study unique rock formations in a remote area. _____.

A) Using sophisticated instruments, they studied the rock formations

B) Sophisticated geologists using instruments studied the rock formations!

C) The rock formations studied were by them using sophisticated instruments.

D) Using sophisticated instruments the rock formations, were studied by them.

4. Excerpt from *The Yellow Wallpaper* by Charlotte Perkins Gilman: *"For the past few months, it _____*

around him that something was not quite right. The changes were subtle at first, but they became more pronounced with time."

A) became evidence to everyone

B) becomes evidence to everyone

C) had become evident to everyone

D) is becoming evident to everyone

5. As the sun rose over the horizon, the photographer set up her camera. She aimed to capture the perfect shot of the landscape. _____ and the beauty of nature inspired her.

A) But it was early,

B) Many were still asleep,

C) How she felt energize,

D) The colors were vibrant,

6. The members of CERN, representing diverse countries and expertise, collaborate across national boundaries to further _____ physics. This cooperative effort aims to enhance global knowledge and foster innovation in the field.

A) her understanding of particle

B) it's understood of particle

C) their understanding of particle

D) theirs understanding of particle

7. The exploration of various voting systems and methods for electing representatives is reshaping democratic processes worldwide. This important topic _____ engagement and influencing electoral outcomes.

A. has been enhancing citizen

B. are enhancing citizen

C. was enhancing citizen

D. have been enhancing citizen

B. Transitions: Select the correct answer that completes the text with the most logical transition.

1. _____ the novel will explore the protagonist's inner conflicts deeply, or it will focus on external events and their impacts on the narrative. Neither approach is inherently superior; it depends on the author's thematic goals and the message they wish to convey.

A) If   B) Either

C) Both   D) Despite

2. The classic prose of Charles Dickens often critiques social injustices of his time, highlighting the struggles of the underprivileged. _____, his novels provide a detailed portrayal of Victorian society's problems and reforms, making them timeless in their relevance.

A) Yet   B) In fact

C) If   D) Nevertheless

3. The geographical features of the Himalayas are awe-inspiring and diverse, attracting adventurers and scientists alike. _____, they play a crucial role in regulating the climate of the surrounding regions, influencing weather patterns and ecosystems.

A) Moreover   B) However

C) Instead   D) What if

4. The emergence of flash fiction as a literary form has been transformative, offering concise narratives that leave a lasting impression. _____ its ability to convey deep emotions and ideas in a limited word count, it has gained popularity among writers and readers alike.

A) What if   B) Despite

C) Even though   D) Because of

5. The Hubble Space Telescope has provided unprecedented images of distant galaxies, expanding our knowledge of the universe and our place within it. _____, its observations have contributed to the study of dark matter and dark energy, opening new avenues for research in astrophysics.

A) Additionally   B) However

C) Instead   D) As was previously stated

6. The study of the distribution of life on Earth has revealed significant patterns in biodiversity, influencing our understanding of ecosystems and conservation. _____, it also highlights the effects of environmental changes on species and habitats worldwide.

A) To resume   B) Furthermore

C) In contrast   D) To get back to the point

C. Punctuation & Boundaries: Select the correct answer from the options provided.

1. The student's outstanding performance in the class earned them a spot on the _____ reflecting not only their hard work but also their dedication to academic excellence. This achievement was a proud moment for both the student and their family.

A) Dean's List,   B) Deans List,

C) Dean List,   D) Deans" List,

2. The event was held on June 5 _____ many attendees had marked on their calendars. This particular day was significant, as it featured guest speakers and activities that everyone looked forward to.

A) ; a date that   B) , a date that

C) a date that   D) : a date that

3. The coach emphasized three key strategies for winning the _____ defense, effective communication, and teamwork. Each player must contribute to achieve victory, as this collaborative effort fosters unity and enhances overall performance.

A) game: strong   B) game-strong

C) game/strong   D) game strong

Test 40

A. Sentence Form and Structure

Select the choice that conforms to the conventions of Standard English.

1. Excerpt from *The Bluest Eye* by Toni Morrison: *"On a bright and crisp autumn morning, as the leaves _____, she felt a sense of calm and clarity that had long eluded her. It was a perfect day, and for the first time in months, she felt hopeful."*

A) cover the paths' ahead

B) were covering the path ahead

C) covered the path's ahead

D) had covered the paths ahead

2. Figurative language enhances the imagery in poetry. _____ metaphors, similes, and personification, poets create vivid pictures in the minds of their readers, allowing emotions and ideas to resonate more deeply.

A) Methods such as the ones

B) Poet using cool techniques

C) Which they do all the time,

D) With the help of

3. The Dead Sea, known for _____ content, has been a source of minerals since ancient times, attracting travelers and scholars alike who marvel at its unique properties and the striking landscapes that surround it.

A) it's extremely high salt

B) its extremely high salt

C) their extreme high salt

D) there extreme high salt

4. In Mark Twain's works, irony _____ to expose the hypocrisies of society and _____ by readers as both humorous and thought-provoking, prompting reflection on the contradictions inherent in human behavior and societal norms.

A) used effectively / has been interpreted

B) could be used effectively / would be interpreted

C) is used effectively / is interpreted

D) uses effectively / interpreted

5. *"We must learn to live together as brothers or perish together as fools."* This message _____, resonating deeply as the world grows smaller and more interconnected. In an age where our fates are intertwined, the call for unity and understanding becomes a clarion call, imploring us to rise above our differences and embrace our shared humanity.

A) becomes more urgent with each passing day

B) is becoming most urgent with each passing day

C) became most urgent with each passing day

D) had become more urgent with each passing day

6. Biochemistry focuses on _____

A) chemical processes, molecular interactions, and how cells functionality

B) chemical processes, molecules interact, and cells functioning.

C) processes that are chemical, interactions that are molecular, and cellular functions.

D) chemical processes, interacting molecules, and cellular functions.

7. If a historian were to document _____ own life, _____ would likely emphasize the major events that shaped _____ understanding of the world, offering insights into personal growth and the broader historical context that influenced their experiences.

A) their; they; their

B) his; his; his

C) one's; one; ones

D) our; we; theirs

B. Idioms

Select the correct answer from the options provided.

1. Instead of focusing on realistic goals that could lead her to success, she spent her time _____, dreaming of unrealistic achievements that were unlikely to ever materialize, which left her feeling unfulfilled and distracted from her true potential.

A) making a plan

B) setting priorities

C) making castles in the air

D) with both feet on the ground

2. The customized workout plan, meticulously designed by a professional trainer, was _____ for the athlete's specific needs, addressing their strengths and weaknesses, and ultimately helping them reach peak performance in their sport.

A) one-size-fits-all

B) tailor-made

C) a bad fit

D) poorly designed

3. The rival presidential candidates, known for their fierce competition and contrasting ideologies, were constantly _____, engaging in heated debates and personal attacks during the campaign, which captivated the media and the electorate alike.

A) seeing eye to eye

B) at each other's throats

C) supporting one another

D) on the same page

4. The politician's public image was a carefully crafted facade; behind the scenes, they were _____, engaging in unethical practices that contradicted their public statements and undermined the trust of their constituents.

A) sailing under false colors

B) staying true to their word

C) winning public support

D) maintaining integrity

5. Looking back at their carefree college years, filled with laughter and camaraderie, they fondly reminisced about those _____ filled with fun, friendship, and endless possibilities, moments that shaped their identities and created lasting memories.

A) hard knocks

B) salad days

C) stressful moments

D) bitter experience

C. Missing Words: Select the correct answer from the options provided.

Dramatic irony is a powerful literary device that occurs when the audience knows more about a situation than the characters do. This technique is often used to create a sense of (1) _____ (clarity, confusion, boredom, suspense) in a narrative, as viewers anticipate the unfolding events with greater awareness of the impending consequences. In many tragic works, dramatic irony intensifies the emotional impact, as characters make decisions based on (2) _____ (knowledge, misunderstandings, certainty, ignorance) of their circumstances.

For example, when a character confidently approaches their fate while the audience knows the tragic outcome, it evokes a profound sense of (3) _____ (tension, relief, joy, indifference). This technique not only enriches the storyline but also highlights the themes of (4) _____ (fate, frippery, trifle, pettiness), as characters grapple with their lack of awareness in a world rife with inevitable outcomes.

Test 41

A. Sentence Form and Structure

Select the choice that conforms to the conventions of Standard English.

1. When a psychologist studies behavior, it is essential that _____ must consider both the biological and environmental factors that influence _____ subjects. Understanding how genetics, brain chemistry, and social contexts interact is crucial for developing a comprehensive view of human behavior.

A) they; their 　　　　　B) one; once

C) he; his 　　　　　　　D) we; our

2. A set of equations, which includes both linear and quadratic forms, _____ solve the problem efficiently and find the correct solutions. This mathematical framework is critical for analyzing complex scenarios and deriving meaningful conclusions, especially in fields such as engineering and economics.

A) were require to 　　　B) are require to

C) has required to 　　　D) is required to

3. Excerpt from a novel: *"The man in black fled across the desert, and the gunslinger _____ determination that echoed in his every step. His shadow stretched out behind him, long and thin as the sun sank lower in the sky, casting an eerie glow over the parched landscape. Each footfall resonated with the weight of fate, as the horizon beckoned with promises of confrontation and destiny."*

A) had followed, drive by a relentless

B) followed, driven by a relentless

C) follows, drove by a relentless

D) was following, driving by a relentless

4. Excerpt from an appreciative and formal text: *"The Sistine Chapel ceiling, painted by Michelangelo between 1508 and 1512, __ of High Renaissance art, exemplifying the mastery of technique and the depth of human emotion captured in each figure. This monumental work not only showcases artistic brilliance but also reflects the cultural and spiritual aspirations of its time."*

A) is pretty much the most amazing thing you'll ever see and

B) showcases some of the best doodles from the Renaissance and

C) is considered a cornerstone

D) really shows off Michelangelo's mad skills and.

5. DNA's double helix structure in 1953, _____ Watson and Crick, revolutionized the field of genetics, fundamentally altering our understanding of heredity and biological processes.

A) discovered by 　　　　B) being discovered for

C) which discovered by 　D) a discovery for

6. The Meiji Restoration of 1868 _____ in Japan, transforming it into a major world power. This pivotal event marked a turning point in Japanese history, leading to significant changes in political structure, economic practices, and social norms.

A) initiates rapid modernization and Westernization

B) initiates rapids modernization and Westernization

C) initiated rapid modernization and Westernization

D) initiate rapid modernization and Westernization

7. The annual science fair showcased impressive projects from students of all ages, attracting the attention of parents, teachers, and community members alike. As they walked through the exhibits, _____ the creativity and effort displayed, highlighting the hard work put in by the students and fostering a spirit of encouragement and appreciation for scientific inquiry.

A) because the students did ok, and they praise

B) even though some were simple, and they praise

C) the judges were strict, and they praised

D) many were captivated, and they praised

B. Transitions: Select the correct answer that completes the text with the most logical transition.

1. The Constitution safeguards individual rights and freedoms, ensuring that citizens are protected against government overreach. _____ these protections are also essential for maintaining a healthy democracy and encouraging civic engagement.

A) Exclusive of   B) Not only this, but

C) Apart from   D) Excluding

2. _____, I've never been a fan of public speaking. The thought of standing in front of a crowd and addressing them fills me with dread. I find it difficult to articulate my thoughts clearly, and I often feel self-conscious and anxious.

A) In spite of   B) Lastly

C) In all honesty   D) In conclusion

3. _____, I've never been particularly fond of horror movies. I find the suspense and tension to be too much for me, and I often find myself covering my eyes or looking away from the screen. But even so, I occasionally watch them out of curiosity or a desire to challenge myself. I've learned that while I may not enjoy the experience, it can be a valuable way to test my limits and confront my fears.

A) Unless   B) To tell the truth

C) Perhaps   D) In contrast

4. The narrative of the five-hour-long documentary is compelling and richly detailed, captivating viewers from the start. _____, its length may be daunting for some, potentially limiting its audience.

A) However   B) Furthermore

C) Additionally   D) Likewise

5. The literature of the Beat Generation has transformed our understanding of rebellion and nonconformity, offering unique perspectives on societal norms. _____, it continues to inspire new generations of writers and thinkers who challenge conventional values.

A) Moreover   B) Somewhat

C) But   D) Yet

6. The rapid growth of urban areas has led to economic development and innovation, driving progress in various sectors. _____, it has also resulted in environmental degradation and social inequality, raising concerns about sustainability and equity.

A) Dismissing   B) If

C) On the other hand   D) Therefore

C. Punctuation & Boundaries: Select the correct answer from the options provided.

1. In her speech, she stated, "*Education is the most powerful weapon which you can use to change the* _____ It resonated with many who value learning and personal growth and highlighted the importance of knowledge.

A) world"   B) world"

C) world."   D) world,"

2. The _____ antics entertained the whole family, bringing laughter and joy to our home. Its curious nature often led to amusing situations, making it a beloved companion. Pets often become cherished members of the family.

A) cat is playful   B) cat's playful

C) cats' playful   D) cats playful

3. The _____ facility offers various programs for students, aiming to enhance learning through innovative technologies. Such resources are invaluable for modern education, providing tools that prepare students for future challenges.

A) stateoftheart   B) 'state of the art"

C) state of the art   D) state-of-the-art

Test 42

A. Sentence Form and Structure
Select the choice that conforms to the conventions of Standard English.

1. The study of economic indicators, such as GDP and unemployment rates, provides crucial insight into a nation's economic health. Understanding these metrics allows policymakers, economists, and investors to gauge current conditions and make informed decisions. _____ economic trends, enabling stakeholders to prepare for potential shifts in the economic landscape.

A) They tend to use to predict future

B) These indicators are used to predict future

C) Analyzing such data may be use to predict future

D) Often those are not used to predict future

2. The ancient Romans built _____ connected the vast empire, facilitating trade, military movement, and cultural exchange across diverse regions. This extensive network of roads was a testament to their engineering prowess and played a crucial role in the cohesion of the empire.

A) their roads, which   B) theirs roads, which

C) they're roads, which D) there roads, which

3. Excerpt from a novel: *"I had seen little of Holmes lately. My marriage had drifted us away from each other, and he _____, and sometimes dangerous, cases that had always captivated him, immersing himself in the mysteries that danced tantalizingly at the edges of his mind. Each new challenge seemed to draw him further into the shadows of London."*

A) had become more interested in the strange

B) becomes more interested in strange

C) is becoming more interested in the strange

D) was become more interested in strange

4. The United Nations strives to _____

A) maintain international peace, promote human rights, and foster cooperation among nations.

B) maintain, promote international peace human rights, and it fosters cooperation among nations.

C) for maintaining international peace human rights promotion, and fostering cooperation among nations.

D) maintaining international peace, promoting human and cooperation rights among nations should be fostered.

5. Having just finished writing the poem, _____.

A) the poet published in a prestigious magazine, felt a sense of pride.

B) it was published in a prestigious magazine, the poet felt a sense of pride.

C) the poet felt a sense of pride, as it was published in a prestigious magazine

D) it was published in a prestigious magazine the poet felt a sense of pride,

6. Excerpt from a news article: *"The Dead Sea, a Salt Lake bordered by Jordan to the east and Israel to the west, _____ on Earth due to its high salt concentration."*

A) is so salty you'll be afloat like a cork and

B) is known as one of the saltiest bodies of water

C) makes for a really weird swimming experience

D) is basically nature's own flotation tank

7. If she _____ she would have passed the exam. With more dedication, the outcome could have been different.

A) study hard,

B) studies hard

C) had studied harder,

D) was studying harder,

B. Idioms

Select the correct answer from the options provided.

1. Despite the palpable tension in the room, where everyone seemed anxious and on edge, she maintained _____, giving no indication of her thoughts or feelings, which allowed her to navigate the situation with an air of calm and control.

A) a poker face

B) wore her heart on her sleeve

C) a friendly smile

D) a relaxed posture

2. The excited child, overflowing with enthusiasm about the upcoming surprise party, couldn't contain their excitement and _____, unintentionally revealing the secret to the very person it was meant to surprise.

A) kept it a secret

B) let the cat out of the bag

C) played coy

D) hold their tongue

3. While the cheaper product was tempting and seemed like an attractive option at first glance, I remembered the old adage, "_____," and opted for the higher-quality item, knowing that it would serve me better in the long run.

A) money talks

B) a penny saved is a penny earned

C) you get what you pay for

D) look before you leap

4. As summer vacation was coming to an end and the excitement of a new school year loomed on the horizon, it was time for the students to _____ and prepare for the upcoming challenges, settling down to review their materials and get organized.

A) enjoy their time

B) crack a book

C) take a break

D) relax more

5. The charity received donations _____, trickling in sporadically rather than in hefty batches, which made it increasingly difficult for them to fund their large-scale projects and initiatives effectively.

A) in large sums

B) flooding in

C) all at once

D) in dribs and drabs

C. Missing Words: Select the correct answer from the options provided.

Scriptwriting is a complex art form that involves the careful construction of various elements to create a compelling narrative for the stage or screen. At the heart of any script lies (1) _____ (dialogue, narration, exposition, monologue), the verbal exchanges between characters that propel the plot forward and reveal character depth. Effective dialogue should not only sound authentic but also serve to (2) _____ (develop, hinder, confuse, obscure) the story by providing essential information, creating conflict, and building relationships.

To guide the performance, scriptwriters incorporate (3) _____ (character names, stage directions, plot summaries, settings), which provide vital visual and auditory cues, as well as character actions and emotions. Furthermore, the evolution of characters is essential to a compelling narrative; therefore, well-crafted scripts include (4) _____ (minor details, static roles, flat characters, character arcs), demonstrating how characters undergo transformation or growth throughout the story.

Test 43

A. Sentence Form and Structure

Select the choice that conforms to the conventions of Standard English.

1. Excerpt from a novel: *"The crowd moved and swayed, and above it all, there was a curious stillness, as if the city itself _____ to happen. A palpable tension hung in the air, thick with anticipation, as the whispers of the gathered masses mingled with the distant sounds of life, creating a moment suspended in time, charged with the promise of change."*

A) had held it breath, waiting for something

B) holds its breath, waiting for something

C) held its breath, waiting for something

D) is holding it breath, waiting for something

2. In dialogue writing, the ability to create realistic and engaging conversations is vital for character development. _____ authentic dialogue can reveal their motivations and enhance the overall narrative, making stories more relatable and impactful for readers who seek to connect with the characters on a deeper level.

A) They shows how   B) It shows how

C) Him shows how   D) Its shows how

3. The concept of opportunity cost in decision-making _____ in economics, helping individuals and businesses make informed choices. Understanding this principle allows for better resource allocation and prioritization of options based on potential benefits and trade-offs, ultimately guiding smarter investments and strategies.

A) are crucial   B) have been crucial

C) has been crucial   D) were crucial

4. Excerpt from a scholarly article: *"The Mayan calendar, known for its cyclical nature and complex system of time measurement, _____ sophisticated understanding of astronomy and mathematics, reflecting the advanced intellect of a civilization that thrived long before modern science took shape."*

A) shows that these ancient folks were seriously smart cookies with a

B) demonstrates the Mayan civilization's

C) proves that Mayans were way ahead of their time when it came to

D) is a mind-bending system that'll make your head spin with its

5. The effects of pollution on ecosystems, such as loss of biodiversity and degradation of habitats, _____ leading to widespread calls for immediate action to protect the environment. This urgent reality has sparked movements and initiatives aimed at restoring balance and preserving the planet for future generations.

A) is alarming,   B) are alarming,

C) has been alarming,   D) was alarming,

6. When writing a research paper, _____ should make sure to cite all sources, so _____ work is credible and trustworthy. Proper citation is essential in academic writing, as it acknowledges the contributions of others and enhances the integrity of one's own research, fostering a culture of respect and intellectual honesty.

A) one; one's   B) we; our

C) he; his   D) they; their

7. The causes and consequences of the Rwandan genocide _____ extensively by historians, and its lessons _____ as crucial for preventing future atrocities. These findings highlight the importance of understanding past events to avoid repeating similar mistakes in the future.

A) are studying / view

B) studied / could be viewed

C) have been studied / are viewed

D) were studied / are viewing

B. Transitions: Select the correct answer that completes the text with the most logical transition.

1. The Romantic poets often emphasized emotion and individual experience in their work, celebrating the beauty of nature and personal introspection. _____, their predecessors in the Enlightenment focused more on reason and empirical evidence, advocating for logic and scientific inquiry as the primary means of understanding the world.

A) Likewise   B) Additionally

C) In contrast   D) Similarly

2. The study of moral development in children explores how individuals learn to distinguish right from wrong and the factors influencing this process. _____ it has taken years of research to fully understand these dynamics, these findings have significantly advanced our knowledge of ethical behavior and decision-making in youth.

A) While   B) Therefore

C) Besides   D) If

3. In classic literature, the portrayal of heroes often aligns with traditional virtues and moral ideals, depicting figures who embody courage, honor, and integrity. _____ in contemporary novels, characters may embody more complex and ambiguous traits, reflecting the nuanced realities of human experience and moral ambiguity that challenge conventional notions of heroism.

A) Similarly   B) Consequently

C) Despite this   D) Whereas

4. The physical properties of gases are well-described by the ideal gas law, which simplifies their behavior under various conditions. _____, liquids and solids require more complex models to account for their interactions and behaviors.

A) Unless   B) Therefore

C) Conversely   D) Furthermore

5. The northern lights are a beautiful phenomenon that attracts many tourists to polar regions, captivating viewers with their vibrant colors and dynamic displays. _____, they offer scientists valuable insights into the Earth's magnetosphere and solar activity.

A) However   B) Even more

C) Maybe   D) Despite this

6. The principles of democracy emphasize the importance of equal representation and individual rights, ensuring that all voices are heard in the political process. _____, these values underpin the stability and fairness of democratic societies, fostering an environment where citizens can participate actively and equitably in governance.

A) Nevertheless   B) In conclusion

C) Above all   D) As a consequence

C. Punctuation & Boundaries: Select the correct answer from the options provided.

1. According to Smith (2015), "The rise of streaming services has transformed the way we consume various forms of entertainment, allowing for greater accessibility and personalization of _____ However, traditional cable still holds a significant audience, particularly among older demographics who prefer familiar programming" (p. 45).

A) media...   B) media'

C) media-   D) media/

2. _____ theorem states that in a right-angled triangle, the square of the hypotenuse is equal to the sum of the squares of the other two sides.

A) Pythagoras"   B) Pythagoras'

C) Pythagoras's   D) Pythagora's

3. Despite its name, the _____ bear, a marsupial native to _____ is not actually a bear. This common misconception often leads to confusion, as these adorable creatures have their own unique characteristics and behaviors.

A) koala / Australia,   B) koala; / Australia,

C) koala, / Australia;   D) koala: / Australia.

Test 44

A. Sentence Form and Structure
Select the choice that conforms to the conventions of Standard English.

1. The renowned pianist's performance was so captivating that it _____ from the audience, a testament to their profound admiration and appreciation for his extraordinary talent. The intricate melodies, the emotional depth, and the technical brilliance of his playing resonated with the audience on a deep level.

A) receives standing ovation

B) receiving standing ovation

C) receive standing ovations

D) received standing ovations

2. The scientists _____ renewable energy sources for over five years now. The ongoing nature of their work is important in addressing environmental challenges.

A) have been conducting their research on

B) conducted their research on

C) conduct their research on

D) are conducting their research on

3. The invention of the transistor transformed electronics. After _____ of electronic devices became possible, leading to the development of modern technology as we know it today.

A) they did that, the miniaturization

B) it is made, the miniaturization

C) this crucial development at Bell Labs, the miniaturization

D) electronics started, the miniaturization

4. Postcolonial literature _____ significantly by the impact of colonialism, with themes of identity and resistance often _____ in the narrative. This genre investigates the complexities of culture and power dynamics in a postcolonial context.

A) influenced / explored

B) has been influenced / explored

C) was influenced / could explore

D) has influenced / was explored

5. In the finance seminar, the guest speaker encouraged _____ to consider the long-term implications of _____ financial policies. It emphasized the importance of thoughtful analysis in financial decision-making.

A) us, ours

B) we, our

C) we, ours

D) us, our

6. The Bayeux Tapestry, a 230-foot-long embroidered cloth, depicts the events leading up to the Norman conquest of England. _____ valuable insights into 11th-century life and warfare, showcasing the artistry and historical significance of this artifact.

A) Its intricate scenes provide

B) It's intricate scenes providing

C) Their intricate scene provided

D) There intricate scene provides

7. Strategically built, the medieval castle was well-defended against invaders. _____. This construction not only provided security but also symbolized power and stability in the region.

A) Strong defense surrounded by a moat was provided against invaders

B) It provided strong defense against invaders surrounded by a moat!

C) The medieval castle surrounded by a moat provided strong defense against invaders

D) Against, the invaders the medieval castle provided strong defense surrounded by a moat.

B. Idioms

Select the correct answer from the options provided.

1. After days of dealing with unruly children who seemed to test her patience at every turn, the babysitter was nearly _____ by the end of the day, feeling as though she had reached her limit and might lose her composure if one more tantrum erupted.

A) round the twist

B) clear-headed

C) level-headed

D) on the wagon

2. Despite losing their job unexpectedly and facing the uncertainty that came with it, they managed to _____, quickly finding new employment opportunities that suited their skills and experience, allowing them to regain their footing.

A) land on their face

B) hit rock bottom

C) fall on their feet

D) come a cropper

3. The teacher, recognizing that everyone has off days and wanting to foster a supportive environment, decided to _____ the student's tardiness this time, but firmly warned them not to make a habit of it, emphasizing the importance of punctuality.

A) follow through

B) take action

C) address the issue

D) let slide

4. By criticizing the company's main product during the team meeting, the employee was essentially _____, jeopardizing not only their own job security but also the overall morale of the team.

A) making a living

B) securing a steady income

C) earning a fortune

D) quarreling with his bread and butter

5. The job applicant was filled with anticipation and anxiety, _____ while waiting for the callback to inform them whether they had been selected for the position, each passing minute heightening their nerves and hopes.

A) at ease

B) on pins and needles

C) calm and collected

D) cool as a cucumber

C. Missing Words: Select the correct answer from the options provided.

Intelligence is a multifaceted concept that has been studied extensively through various theories and frameworks. One prominent theory is Howard Gardner's (1) _____ (multiple intelligences, emotional intelligence, fluid intelligence, creative intelligence), which suggests that individuals possess different types of intelligence, such as linguistic, logical-mathematical, and interpersonal. Traditionally, intelligence has often been measured through (2) _____ (fitness tests, personality assessments, IQ testing, performance evaluations), which aims to quantify cognitive abilities.

However, critics argue that these tests may not capture the full (3) _____ (simplicity, uniformity, predictability, spectrum) of human intelligence, as they often overlook creative and practical skills. Moreover, the interpretation of IQ scores can lead to (4) _____ (clarity, consensus, misunderstandings, approval) about an individual's potential, raising important questions about how we define and value intelligence in society.

Test 45

A. Sentence Form and Structure

Select the choice that conforms to the conventions of Standard English.

1. The geography of a region can significantly impact its economy in various ways, such as by determining the availability of natural resources. _____ agriculture, and transportation.

A) Which is influence trade,

B) These factors influence trade,

C) Being shaped by influences trade,

D) For example, influenced trade,

2. Statistics, when interpreted accurately and in context, can _____ into complex phenomena such as social behavior, economic trends, and scientific research, allowing for better decision-making and understanding.

A. provide invaluable insights

B. provides invaluable insight

C. is providing invaluable insights

D. are providing invaluable insight

3. When analyzing argumentative essays, it is crucial to evaluate multiple aspects. _____

A) The evidence is strong, the thesis is assessed.

B) Evaluating evidence the strength, of the thesis is assessed.

C) The thesis is assessed, evidence strength is evaluated for.

D) The strength of the thesis is assessed, and the evidence is evaluated.

4. A mathematician was working on something innovative, and in his quest for new ideas, he found his muse. _____.

A) Inspired by nature's patterns, he developed a new theory

B) He developed, a new theory inspired by nature's patterns

C) The new theory was inspired by nature's patterns, developed by him.

D) Inspired by nature's patterns a new theory, was developed by him.

5. A multitude of literary devices, which encompass various techniques such as metaphors, similes, and personification, _____ by authors to craft vivid imagery and convey deeper meanings within their texts.

A. is skillfully employed

B. has been skillfully employed

C. are skillfully employed

D. have been skillfully employ

6. The philosopher Socrates, renowned for his method of questioning known as the Socratic method, is widely regarded as one of the foundational figures in Western philosophy. He was truly an influential thinker, _____, encouraged critical thinking and intellectual honesty as essential components of philosophical inquiry.

A) who was in ancient Athens

B) whose ideas have shaped Western thought

C) being a champ of knowledge and virtue

D) that challenge traditional belief

7. The unification of Italy in 1861, a significant historical event _____ and leadership of prominent figures such as Garibaldi and Cavour, successfully created a single nation-state from a diverse collection of independent kingdoms.

A) led by the efforts

B) being led by the effort

C) leading by the effort

D) which lead by the efforts

B. Transitions: Select the correct answer that completes the text with the most logical transition.

1. Despite the overwhelming odds and the seemingly insurmountable challenges, the explorers pressed on, their determination unwavering. They knew that turning back would mean abandoning their mission, their dreams, and the hope of making a difference. With every step, they faced new obstacles, _____, they refused to give up.

A) What if　　　　　　B) As was stated

C) but even so　　　　D) firstly

2. Economic geography examines the spatial distribution of financial activity, revealing patterns and trends that shape local and global economies. _____, it also highlights significant disparities in wealth and resources that continue to challenge policymakers, prompting ongoing discussions about equity and development.

A) Furthermore　　　　B) To resume

C) Initially　　　　　　D) In consequence

3. The discoveries of ancient civilizations provide invaluable insights into early human societies, enriching our understanding of history. _____, much of their knowledge has been lost or remains incomplete due to the passage of time, posing challenges for historians and archaeologists.

A) In the event that　　B) Nonetheless

C) With this intention　　D) For the purpose of

4. _____ the weather was harsh and the terrain was challenging, the mountaineers persevered in their ascent to the summit. Driven by their unwavering determination and fueled by their shared passion for exploration, they faced every obstacle with courage and resilience, ultimately reaching their goal and standing triumphantly atop the mountain peak.

A) Although　　　　　　B) But

C) In the case of　　　　D) Contrarily

5. _____ many early astronomers were limited by their observational tools, their theories laid the foundation for modern astronomy, inspiring future generations of scientists. Subsequent discoveries have built upon these initial ideas to further our understanding of the universe.

A) Eventually　　　　　B) Incidentally

C) Though　　　　　　D) Under those circumstances

6. The theory of plate tectonics explains many geological phenomena, such as earthquakes and volcanic activity, providing a comprehensive framework for understanding Earth's dynamics. _____, it does not account for all geological features, and other processes must be considered to gain a complete picture of the planet's geology.

A) Next　　　　　　　　B) Because of this

C) However　　　　　　D) That being the case

C. Punctuation & Boundaries: Select the correct answer from the options provided.

1. What role do neurotransmitters play in communication between neurons in the _____ This question probes into the intricate processes that allow our brain to function, affecting everything from mood to movement. Understanding these chemicals is crucial for insights into neurological health.

A) human brain,　　　　B) human brain

C) human brain!　　　　D) human brain?

2. _____ Archimedes' famous exclamation upon discovering the principle of buoyancy while taking a bath illustrates the joy of scientific discovery. This moment of inspiration led to significant advancements in physics and engineering.

A) Eureka"　　　　　　B) Eureka

C) Eureka-　　　　　　D) Eureka!

3. The survey needs to be completed by _____, ensuring that all responses are collected in a timely manner for analysis. Meeting this deadline is essential for the project's success.

A) 08 10 2024　　　　　B) 08/10/2024

C) 08"10"2024　　　　　D) 08,10,2024

Test 46

A. Sentence Form and Structure

Select the choice that conforms to the conventions of Standard English.

1. The human heart, a muscular organ _____, pumps blood throughout the body, ensuring the delivery of oxygen and nutrients to vital organs. Its rhythmic contractions, often described as a heartbeat, are essential for maintaining life and sustaining bodily functions.

A) which is somewhere in the thoracic cavities

B) whose rhythm is controlled by electrical impulses

C) being like a complex and efficient pump

D) that can be affected by various diseases

2. Neither the Aztecs nor the Incas could have possibly foreseen the profound and transformative impact that _____ with European explorers would have on their civilizations.

A) their encounters   B) its encounters

C) his encounter   D) her encounter

3. *"It is not in the stars to hold our destiny but in ourselves."* He _____ that it had become a mantra of sorts, a belief that guided his every decision. Each repetition imbued him with a sense of agency, reminding him that the power to shape his fate rested firmly within his grasp, illuminating his path through the shadows of uncertainty.

A) repeats this phrase so many times

B) repeated this phrase so many times

C) had repeated this phrase so many times

D) was repeating this phrase so many times

4. The Treaty of Westphalia, signed in 1648, marked a significant turning point in European history by officially _____. This agreement not only concluded a prolonged period of conflict but also established the modern concept of state sovereignty, fundamentally reshaping the political landscape of Europe.

A) ended the devastating Thirty Years' War

B) ends the devastating Thirty Years' War

C) it ended the devastating Thirty Years' War

D) ending the devastating Thirty Years' War

5. Greek mythology is renowned for its rich tapestry of narratives. It is especially notable for its _____.

A) powerful heroic gods mortals, and stories that inspire.

B) powerful gods, heroic mortals, and inspiring stories

C) gods that were powerful, mortals who were heroic, and stories inspiring

D) gods that are powerful, heroic mortals, and stories that inspire

6. Excerpt from a novel: *"And so, we beat on, boats against the current, borne back ceaselessly into the past. For years, he _____ a moment, a place, a feeling that had long since disappeared, striving against the relentless tide of time. Each effort was a desperate attempt to grasp the intangible, to revive a fleeting joy that seemed forever out of reach, echoing through the corridors of his memory."*

A) was pouring his entire being into recreating

B) pours his entire being into recreating

C) poured his entire being into recreating

D) had poured his entire being into recreating

7. Stonehenge, an iconic prehistoric monument located in England, has captivated the imagination of historians and archaeologists alike for centuries. Despite extensive research and numerous theories, the exact purpose behind _____ remains a topic of ongoing debate and speculation among scholars and enthusiasts.

A) its construction   B) it's construction

C) their construction   D) there construction

B. Idioms

Select the correct answer from the options provided.

1. The couple's relationship, once filled with love and understanding, had turned into _____, characterized by constant arguing and bickering over the smallest of issues, leading to a strained atmosphere that made it difficult for them to communicate effectively.

A) peaceful coexistence

B) harmonious union

C) a cat and dog life

D) birds of a feather

2. Finding a specific document in the disorganized office, where papers were strewn about haphazardly and nothing was in its rightful place, was like looking for a _____, testing my patience and determination as I sifted through the chaos.

A) needle in a haystack

B) book on a shelf

C) coin in a fountain

D) jack the lad

3. Implementing the new company policy would undoubtedly cause some initial disruptions and pushback from employees, but the management believed that _____. Understanding that progress often requires sacrifice and adjustment.

A) you can't make an omelet without breaking eggs

B) every cloud has a silver lining

C) all good things come to an end

D) easy come, easy go

4. Trying to convince my stubborn friend to change their mind about the movie they wanted to see was like _____; they were completely inflexible and resistant to any alternative suggestions, no matter how persuasive my arguments were.

A) on the same wavelength

B) reasoning with a friend

C) having a heart-to-heart

D) talking to a brick wall

5. The country was caught in a _____ of poverty, where the lack of resources led to poor education and limited job opportunities, creating a cycle of despair that seemed impossible to escape from.

A) upward trend

B) constructive cycle

C) positive feedback loop

D) vicious circle

C. Missing Words: Select the correct answer from the options provided.

Map reading is a fundamental skill that equips individuals with the ability to interpret and derive meaning from geographic representations. A myriad of (1) _____ (numbers, colors, maps, ideas) exist, each tailored to convey specific geographic information. Topographic maps, for example, utilize (2) _____ (shading, colors, symbols, contour lines) to delineate variations in elevation, providing invaluable insights into the terrain's character.

Moreover, map (3) _____ (angles, orientations, projections, placements) are essential for translating the spherical Earth's complex curvature onto a flat surface. Different map projections, such as Mercator and Robinson, present distinct advantages and distortions, necessitating careful consideration for accurate (4) _____ (navigation, decoration, adornment, confusion) and informed decision-making.

Test 47

A. Sentence Form and Structure

Select the choice that conforms to the conventions of Standard English.

1. The Wright brothers, pioneers of aviation, dedicated countless hours to experimenting with flight technology. _____.

A) They flew their first successful airplane using innovative design principles

B) Using successful innovative design principles; the first airplane flew

C) The first successful airplane was using innovative design principles, flown by them

D) Airplane using innovative design principles was flown successfully by them

2. Game theory analyzes _____.

A) strategical decision-making, competitive interactions, and structuring of payoffs

B) strategies in decision-making, interactions competitive, and payoff structures

C) decision-making strategically, competitive interactions, and payoff structures

D) strategic decision-making, competitive interactions, and payoff structures.

3. The Behistun Inscription, a remarkable multilingual text carved into a cliff face in Iran, played a pivotal role in the deciphering of cuneiform script. _____ unlocked new insights, enriching our understanding of ancient Near Eastern civilizations and their histories.

A) Their discovery and subsequent translation

B) It's discovery and subsequent translation

C) Its discovery and subsequent translation

D) There is discovery and subsequent translation

4. The novel delves deeply into profound themes of love and loss, vividly set against the backdrop of a war-torn country. _____ many found themselves emotionally invested in the story, highlighting the powerful connection between the narrative and its audience.

A) As the writing was powerful,

B) But it was fictional,

C) The plot was complicated,

D) Something felt detached,

5. During a chemical reaction, the transformation of reactants into products occurs through a series of intricate processes. _____ forming new bonds, which is fundamental to this transformation, allowing the rearrangement of atoms and the creation of new substances.

A) Where molecules breaking and

B) This process involves breaking and

C) The reactant breaking and

D) Which it results in breaking and

6. Every philosopher within the Stoic tradition emphasized the critical importance of aligning _____ and virtue. This alignment was seen as essential for achieving a harmonious life, grounded in rational thought and ethical behavior.

A) their actions with reasons

B) its action with reason

C) our actions with reason

D) they're action with reasons

7. The Congress of Vienna, convened in 1815, was a significant diplomatic gathering that sought to reshape the political landscape of Europe following the defeat of Napoleon. _____ this congress aimed to establish a new balance of power to prevent future conflicts and maintain stability in the region.

A) Which redraws the map of Europe,

B) Redrawing the map of Europe,

C) Redrew the map of Europe,

D) Redraws the map of Europe,

B. Transitions: Select the correct answer that completes the text with the most logical transition.

1. The choice of point of view is crucial in storytelling, as it shapes how readers perceive characters and events. _____, this decision significantly influences the emotional depth and engagement of the narrative, highlighting the importance of perspective in literary works.

A) In contrast   B) Despite this

C) And if   D) With this in mind

2. The principles of classical physics are well-established and widely accepted, serving as the foundation for much of modern science. _____, they are insufficient to explain phenomena at quantum scales, where new theories are required to enhance our understanding of the universe.

A) Granting that   B) Accordingly

C) Initially   D) And yet

3. The implementation of renewable energy sources will have a significant impact on reducing carbon emissions, contributing to global efforts to combat climate change. _____, it is crucial to address climate change effectively, regardless of the specific strategies employed.

A) Therefore   B) If

C) In spite of   D) Possibly

4. _____ of the cost, I want to buy that new car. Even if it's more expensive than I can afford, I'm determined to purchase that car because I've been dreaming of it for so long.

A) Alternatively   B) Regardless

C) In other words   D) At the very least

5. The secret passage led to a hidden chamber filled with ancient artifacts and documents that offered a glimpse into the forgotten history of the castle. _____, that's what I thought until I discovered the hidden room behind the bookcase. It was as if the castle had been guarding its secrets for centuries, waiting for someone to stumble upon them and uncover the truth.

A) Either way   B) Whether way

C) In either case   D) Or at least

6. _____, whether the negotiations are successful or not, we must remain committed to finding a peaceful resolution to this conflict. The stakes are too high to allow emotions or short-sightedness to dictate our actions. We must approach the situation with empathy, understanding, and a genuine desire to find common ground.

A) Might be   B) At the outset

C) Whichever happens   D) Perchance

C. Punctuation & Boundaries: Select the correct answer from the options provided.

1. After a long day of classes, homework, and extracurricular _____ students feel exhausted. This fatigue can impact their ability to focus and perform well in their studies, highlighting the importance of balance and self-care.

A) activities, many   B) activities many

C) activities: many   D) activities. Many

2. The shocked lottery winner gasped: "_____ I don't know what to say. This is unexpected." This moment of disbelief captured the excitement and surprise that many dream of experiencing when winning the lottery.

A) I.   B) I...

C) I,   D) I-

3. This concert is going to be _____ The band has a fantastic lineup, and the energy will be electric, promising an unforgettable experience for all attendees. Everyone is eagerly anticipating the performance.

A) incredible!   B) incredible

C) incredible...   D) incredible.

Test 48

A. Sentence Form and Structure

Select the choice that conforms to the conventions of Standard English.

1. To put it simply, the Emancipation Proclamation _____,

A) Issued by President Lincoln in 1863, declared all slaves in Confederate states free, marking a turning point in the Civil War and advancing abolition.

B) which was issued by President Lincoln in 1863, it declared that all slaves in Confederate states were to be freed, representing a significant turning point in the Civil War and advancing the abolitionist cause.

C) issued in 1863, it declared the freedom of slaves in Confederate states, marking a major turning point in the Civil War and the advancement of abolition.

D) by President Lincoln's in 1863 declared the freedom of slaves in Confederate states, serving as a turning point in the Civil War and furthering the cause of abolition.

2. Excerpt from an objective passage: *"The Inca civilization, renowned for its remarkable architectural achievements and sophisticated agricultural practices, _____ without the use of wheeled vehicles, iron tools, or a formal writing system."*

A) somehow put together a pretty impressive society

B) managed to build a monumental empire

C) pulled off some amazing stuff

D) showed everyone else up by creating a huge empire

3. Enzymes _____ chemical reactions in living organisms.

A) are biological catalysts that speed up

B) is to facilitate the body's reactions

C) help to speeding up metabolic

D) being proteins enhancing

4. Social perception is a fundamental aspect of human interaction, _____ cognitive processes that help us interpret and understand the behaviors of others. This phenomenon plays a crucial role in shaping our judgments and relationships.

A) enact through various

B) was enacting through varied

C) enacted through various

D) enacting through varied

5. The economics of healthcare is a multifaceted subject that requires careful analysis. Policymakers must consider _____, and quality when designing effective healthcare systems that meet the needs of the population.

A) it cost, accessibility   B) their cost, accessibility

C) its cost, accessibility   D) his cost, accessibility

6. The development of democracy in Ancient Rome _____ model for many modern governments, illustrating the evolution of political systems and the principles of governance that continue to influence the contemporary democratic system.

A) are a significant

B) has been a significant

C) were significant

D) have been significant

7. In a political science debate, each participant must defend _____ position clearly and respond effectively to _____ opponents. This requires not only a strong argument but also the ability to engage with differing viewpoints constructively.

A) his; his

B) their; their

C) one's; one's

D) our; our

B. Idioms

Select the correct answer from the options provided.

1. The latest social media craze, which swept through platforms like wildfire and captivated countless users, had everyone _____, eagerly sharing voluminous posts and videos that reflected the latest trends and challenges.

A) on the bandwagon

B) out-of-touch

C) jumping ship

D) off the bandwagon

2. The company's financial stability, which had once seemed secure and promising, now felt like a _____, with various factors threatening to bring the entire operation crashing down if not addressed promptly.

A) solid foundation

B) safe investment

C) brick wall

D) house of cards

3, After hours of searching for the lost documents, we managed to locate them in the back of a cluttered drawer, _____. The chaos of the office made it nearly impossible to find anything, but our persistence paid off in the end.

A) for a song

B) at a high price

C) with great difficulty

D) for a fortune

4, Dealing with feelings of loneliness, a common struggle that many face in today's fast-paced world, is _____; many people experience similar emotions at some point in their lives, reminding us that we are not alone in our toils.

A) unique to you

B) not unique to you

C) uncommon

D) rare find

5. The early morning bird catches the worm, so I'm always up _____, eager to seize the day and start my morning productively with a fresh mindset and clear goals.

A) late in the evening

B) at the crack of dawn

C) before sunset

D) in the middle of the night

C. Missing Words: Select the correct answer from the options provided.

John Keats is renowned for his rich and evocative poetry that explores profound themes and employs intricate language. One notable aspect of his work is the (1) _____ (structure, randomness, simplicity, brevity) of his poems, often characterized by carefully crafted forms such as sonnets and odes. These structures enhance the musicality and rhythm of his verses. Keats frequently delves into themes of (2) _____ (coldness, chaos, monotony, beauty), reflecting on the transient nature of life and the pursuit of aesthetic experiences. His exploration of love, nature, and mortality creates a deep emotional resonance with readers.

Additionally, Keats's use of (3) _____ (irony, ambiguity, imagery, cliches) is particularly striking; he employs vivid descriptions that engage the senses and evoke strong feelings. Overall, the interplay of (4) _____ (language, noise, silence, confusion) and form in Keats's poetry invites readers to reflect on the complexities of human experience.

Test 49

A. Sentence Form and Structure

Select the choice that conforms to the conventions of Standard English.

1 The role of the setting in *Jane Eyre* by Charlotte Brontë _____ analysis. Researchers explore how the settings reflect the protagonist's inner turmoil and contribute to her development throughout the narrative.

A) have been a topic of much scholar

B) has been a topic of much scholarly

C) are a topic of much scholarly

D) were a topic of much scholar

2. The herd of cattle _____, undisturbed by the passing vehicles, reflecting the harmony of nature amidst the hustle of modern life. Their gentle movements created a picturesque scene, where the simplicity of pastoral existence stood in stark contrast to the frenetic pace of the world beyond the rolling hills.

A) had grazing peacefully in the meadow

B) were graze peacefully into the meadow

C) was grazing peaceful in the meadow

D) are grazed peaceful into the meadow

3. In *The Catcher in the Rye*, Holden Caulfield often struggles with the complex idea of growing up. His experiences in New York City make _____, as he grapples with the challenges and realities of maturity.

A) him increasingly disillusioned with adulthood

B) he increasingly disillusion with adulthood

C) himself increasingly disillusion with adulthood

D) they increasingly disillusioned with adulthood

4. To be concise, the Internet _____.

A) which was developed in the late 20th century; has revolutionized the way in which people communicate and access information.

B) developed in the late 20th century, has revolutionized communication and information access

C) a technology developed towards the end of the 21st century, has brought about a revolution in the ways people communicate and access information.

D) in the late 19th century, lead to revolutionary changes in how people communicate and access information.

5. Excerpt from an enthusiastic and inviting travel brochure: *"Milan is a heaven for foodies and offers an exceptional culinary experience. _____"*

A) The city has a few okay restaurants if you're hungry.

B) Savor the flavors of our vibrant culinary scene!

C) There are some decent places to eat around here.

D) You might want to try the local cuisine.

6. _____ of the oldest pieces of literature, *The Epic of Gilgamesh* provides profound insight into ancient Mesopotamian culture, exploring themes of friendship, mortality, and human experience.

A) Believed to be one

B) If believed to be one

C) Because believed to be ones

D) As believed to be ones

7. The solar system, consisting of the Sun, eight planets, and countless other celestial bodies, is a complex and fascinating system. Our planet, Earth, _____, is the only known celestial body to support life, highlighting its distinctive qualities and delicate balance.

A) that is in the galaxy they call the Milky Way

B) whose distance from the Sun is like just about right

C) being a unique and fragile ecosystem

D) which has been explored by humans and aliens

B. Transitions: Select the correct answer that completes the text with the most logical transition.

1. The study of historical texts provides insights into past societies and their values, revealing the foundations of cultural norms. _____, it is important to consider how these historical perspectives influence modern cultural and social practices, shaping our understanding of identity and tradition.

A) To conclude   B) Incidentally

C) What if   D) Parenthetically

2. The development of renewable energy sources, such as solar and wind power, has significantly reduced our reliance on fossil fuels. Additionally, advancements in energy storage technology have improved the efficiency of renewable energy systems. _____, increasing public awareness and support for sustainable practices have accelerated the transition to a greener future.

A) At least   B) No less than

C) Last but not least   D) By the way

3. _____, let's discuss the recent advancements in renewable energy technology, now that we have talked about the causes. These novel approaches are crucial for addressing climate change. This field has seen significant progress in both efficiency and implementation, offering new solutions for sustainable energy production.

A) Unless   B) So and so

C) Despite   D) Moving forward

4. The narrative explores complex themes of identity and belonging in a multicultural society. _____, the author's personal experiences significantly influenced the development of these characters.

A) Incidentally   B) Afterward

C) Subsequently   D) Previously

5. The project faced numerous challenges and setbacks during its initial stages. _____, with perseverance and innovation, the team was able to overcome these obstacles and achieve remarkable success.

A) Eventually   B) With this in mind

C) Initially   D) In the event that

6. I just finished organizing the community event for this weekend. _____, if you're interested in volunteering, we could really use some extra hands to help set up!

A) Regrettably   B) But even so

C) To begin with   D) By the way

C. Punctuation & Boundaries: Select the correct answer from the options provided.

1. The novel's characters are complex and relatable; they face challenges that mirror _____. Readers often find themselves empathizing with their journeys. This connection enhances the reading experience.

A) real-life struggle's   B) reallife struggles

C) real-life struggles   D) reallife-struggles

2. The fast-paced world of sports requires athletes to be both physically and mentally _____ Training involves rigorous workouts and strategic planning. Success depends on dedication.

A) prepared.   B) prepared:

C) prepared!   D) prepared

3. Socrates is credited with saying, *"The only true wisdom is in knowing you know* _____ This profound statement encourages humility and self-reflection, reminding us that the pursuit of knowledge is a lifelong journey.

A) *nothing"*   B) *nothing.*"

C) *nothing*"   D) *nothing,"*

Test 50

A. Sentence Form and Structure
Select the choice that conforms to the conventions of Standard English.

1. One of the most significant challenges faced by contemporary novelists _____ of diverse perspectives and experiences into their narratives. This task is crucial for reflecting the complexities of modern society.

A. are the effective integration

B. is the effective integration

C. has been the effective integration

D. have been the effective integration

2. The Roswell incident continues to fascinate UFO enthusiasts, despite _____ concrete evidence. This enduring intrigue highlights the power of mythology and speculation in popular culture.

A) his lack of   B) their lack of

C) its lack of   D) her lack of

3. In *The Great Gatsby*, the green light at the end of Daisy's dock symbolizes Gatsby's dreams. _____ he cannot reach it, no matter how hard he tries, emphasizing the theme of longing and disillusionment.

A) But the light is always faint,

B) Yet it is a small beacon,

C) Probably a symbol of hope and desire,

D) However, despite his wealth,

4. Modernism in literature is characterized by _____. This movement reflects the shifting perspectives and complexities of the early 20th century.

A) stream of consciousness writing, fragmented narratives, and themes of alienation

B) writing in a stream of consciousness, narratives fragmented, and alienation as a theme

C) writing that is stream of consciousness, narratives are fragmented, and alienation theme

D) using stream of consciousness, narratives that are fragmented, and alienation themes

5. In environmental science, _____. This field examines the intricate relationships between human activity and the natural world, focusing on sustainability and conservation.

A) the impact of pollution is studied, ecosystems are analyzed

B) ecosystems are analyzed the impact, of pollution is evident

C) pollution is studied, and the impact on ecosystems is analyzed

D) the ecosystems' impact is analyzed, pollution is studied

6. Marie Curie worked assiduously on groundbreaking research. _____.

A) She discovered radium while working tirelessly in her laboratory

B) Working tirelessly in the laboratory radium was discovered by her.

C) Tirelessly working Marie Curie in her laboratory discovered radium

D) Radium was discovered by her working tirelessly in her laboratory.

7. Several eminent scholars of anthropology joined the seminar. The organizers invited _____ to present _____ research on the cultural practices of indigenous communities. This event aimed to foster understanding and appreciation of diverse cultural heritages.

A) they, their

B) them, their

C) their, their

D) themselves, their

B. Idioms

Select the correct answer from the options provided.

1. The crisis team worked frantically against the clock, knowing that every passing minute increased the risk of environmental devastation. They knew they were operating _____, trying to contain the oil spill before it caused irreparable damage to the coastline and the delicate ecosystems it supported.

A) in the nick of time

B) with plenty of time

C) ahead of schedule

D) at the eleventh hour

2. She wanted to quit her job to pursue her passion for travel and adventure, but she realized that you _____, as she needed a steady income to support herself and manage her daily expenses, making the decision much more complicated than she had hoped.

A) can't have your cake and eat it too

B) can have it all

C) can't run before you walk

D) can kill two birds with one stone

3. The experienced thief moved through the house with the utmost caution, knowing that even the slightest sound could alert the occupants; he was _____, carefully avoiding any creaking floorboards or suspicious noises that might give him away.

A) as loud as a lion

B) quiet as a cat

C) gone with the wind

D) noisy as a crowd

4. Despite facing intense pressure from the media and public opinion, the politician remained steadfast in his beliefs and _____ on his controversial stance, refusing to back down or waver in the face of adversity.

A) backed down

B) caved in

C) watered down

D) stood his ground

5. The persistent rumors about the celebrity couple's divorce had been circulating for months, fueled by speculation and gossip, and there was definitely _____; something must have been happening behind the scenes to spark such widespread chatter.

A) a wild goose chase

B) no truth in rumors

C) no need to worry

D) no smoke without fire

C. Missing Words: Select the correct answer from the options provided.

International relations is a complex field that encompasses the interactions between nations, focusing on how they manage their relationships. A key aspect of this discipline is (1) _____ (diplomacy, conflict, isolationism, nationalism), which involves negotiations and dialogue aimed at resolving disputes and fostering cooperation. Diplomacy can take many forms, including bilateral talks between two countries or multilateral discussions involving several nations. In addition to diplomacy, (2) _____ (governmental agencies, local councils, private enterprises, international organizations) play a pivotal role in facilitating cooperation and addressing global challenges.

Organizations such as the United Nations and the World Trade Organization provide platforms for dialogue, promote peace, and establish international norms. These entities help coordinate responses to issues like (3) _____ (economic disparity, local governance, climate change, cultural exchange) and humanitarian crises. Understanding the dynamics of (4) _____ (foreign affairs, domestic policy, cultural studies, economic theory) is essential for analyzing how countries interact on the global stage and the impact of their decisions on world stability.

Test 51

A. Sentence Form and Structure

Select the choice that conforms to the conventions of Standard English.

1. In financial literacy, _____. Mastering this concept is essential for achieving long-term stability and security in personal finances.

A) understanding budgeting is crucial financial security achievement

B) achieving financial security budgeting, is crucial to understand

C) budgeting key is crucial to financial security understanding

D) financial security is achieved by understanding budgeting

2. The Venus de Milo, an ancient Greek statue discovered on the island of Milos, is celebrated for _____ the loss of its arms. This masterpiece continues to captivate art lovers around the world.

A) it's graceful beauty despite

B) its graceful beauty despite

C) their graceful beauty despite

D) there graceful beauty despite

3. The Black Death was a devastating pandemic that swept through Europe in the 14th century. As _____ spread, it caused widespread social and economic upheaval, reshaping societies for generations.

A) they were

B) it was rapidly

C) the disease, caused by the bacterium Yersinia pestis,

D) Europe was dying

4. He usually _____ after school, but today he played basketball first. This change in routine highlights how activities can vary from day to day.

A) do his homeworks right

B) doing his homework right

C) does his homework right

D) did his homeworks right

5. Ocean acidification _____ by increasing CO2 levels, and its effects _____ devastating to marine life. This phenomenon poses a significant threat to coral reefs and other vital ecosystems.

A) is caused / can be

B) has caused / are

C) caused / is

D) causes / could be

6. In literature analysis, when _____ examines the themes of a story, _____ must consider the historical context in which it was written. This understanding enriches the interpretation of the text and its relevance, allowing readers to appreciate the nuances and complexities that shaped the author's perspective, and the societal issues reflected within the narrative.

A) they; they

B) he; he

C) one; one

D) we; we

7. The city council recently implemented a new recycling program to reduce waste and promote sustainability. Since the program started, residents _____ resulting in a significant decrease in landfill waste. This positive change reflects a growing commitment to environmental responsibility.

A) recycle more diligently,

B) have recycled more diligently,

C) had recycled more diligently,

D) are recycling more diligently,

B. Transitions: Select the correct answer that completes the text with the most logical transition.

1. The main argument of the essay is the impact of industrialization on urban development, highlighting the transformation of cities. _____, this focus is crucial for understanding the broader implications of historical changes and their effects on society.

A) Secondly

B) Again

C) In addition

D) Moreover,

2. We discussed the challenges of climate change and the importance of reducing carbon emissions. _____ our original topic, the development of renewable energy sources is crucial in addressing this global crisis.

A) What is more

B) To resume

C) Lastly

D) Initially

3. The initial findings of the study suggested a correlation between increased screen time and lower academic performance. However, upon further analysis, these results were inconclusive. _____, the research did highlight the importance of digital literacy and responsible technology use among young people.

A) Anyhow

B) At the outset

C) To start with

D) Originally

4. The rise in sea levels poses a significant threat to coastal communities worldwide. _____, there is an urgent need for global cooperation to develop and implement effective adaptation strategies.

A) Primarily

B) To begin with

C) Before I go

D) Therefore

5. The increasing frequency and intensity of natural disasters has highlighted the vulnerability of many communities. _____, it is imperative to invest in disaster preparedness and resilience to mitigate the impact of these events.

A) So

B) Fundamentally

C) Despite

D) Fortunately

6. The global economy has experienced significant fluctuations due to factors such as geopolitical tensions, technological advancements, and climate change. _____, navigating the complexities of the modern economic landscape requires a multifaceted approach that considers both short-term challenges and long-term sustainability.

A) Profoundly

B) What if

C) Perhaps

D) In short

C. Punctuation & Boundaries: Select the correct answer from the options provided.

1. The famous opening line of _____ *Anna Karenina* states, *"All happy families are alike; each unhappy family is unhappy in its own way."* This quote encapsulates the complexities of human relationships and the unique struggles that families face.

A) Leo Tolstoys"

B) Leo Tolstoys

C) Leo Tolstoys'

D) Leo Tolstoy's

2. The world's tallest mountain, Mount Everest, reaches a staggering height of _____ above sea level, making it a challenging destination for climbers from around the globe. Its majestic peak attracts adventurers and nature lovers alike.

A) 29,029 feet

B) 29029 feet

C) 29"029 feet

D) 29.029 feet

3. The one-hundred-and-fifty-year-old house had a _____ garden filled with colorful, old-fashioned flowers. This charming space served as a peaceful retreat for the family, showcasing a variety of blooms throughout the seasons.

A) threequarteracre

B) three-quarter-acre

C) three quarter acre

D) three=quarter=acre

Test 52

A. Sentence Form and Structure

Select the choice that conforms to the conventions of Standard English.

1. Existentialism in *The Stranger* by Albert Camus' _____ the meaning of life and the inevitability of death since its publication. This philosophical approach encourages deep reflection on personal existence.

A) have challenged reader to question

B) has challenged readers to question

C) were challenging readers to question

D) are challenging reader to question

2. The Gothic atmosphere in *Wuthering Heights* is heightened by the bleak, desolate setting. _____ of foreboding throughout the novel, enhancing the emotional impact of the character's struggles.

A) It creates a sense

B) They create a sense

C) Its creates a sense

D) Their create a sense

3. Avoiding wordiness, we can define science fiction as a genre _____.

A) that explores imaginative concept, often set in the future and examining the impact of science and technology on society and the human condition.

B) that imagines future societies, showcasing how advancements affect human experiences and challenges

C) that dips into into futuristic themes, reflecting on humanity's relationship with technology and societal change.

D) which examines possible futures and the implications of scientific advancements on

4. When experimenting with chemistry, a scientist must take careful notes to ensure _____ can replicate _____. This practice is essential for maintaining the integrity and reliability of scientific research.

A) they; their results

B) he; his results

C) one; ones results

D) us; our results

5. An excerpt from a friendly and approachable social media post of a company: *"Dear Valued Customer, the wait is finally over.* _____

A) We're happy to announce our new product line, and you should totally buy it."

B) Our new product line is now available, if you're interested!"

C) You need to check out our new product line, it's amazing."

D) We're thrilled to introduce our new product line, and we think you'll love it!"

6. *Moby-Dick*, a novel by Herman Melville, is often _____ and revenge. This literary work delves into profound themes that resonate with readers across generations.

A) describing as a complex exploring of obsession

B) describes as a complex exploring of obsession

C) described as a complex exploration of obsession

D) describe as a complex exploration of obsession

7. Remote sensing, a technology that utilizes satellites and other tools to gather data about the Earth, is vital for various scientific applications. The advanced systems, _____, provide critical insights into environmental changes and resource management.

A) that are line up with geographic features

B) whose capabilities continue to obscure

C) being tools for data dumps

D) which are essential for monitoring ecosystems

B. Idioms

Select the correct answer from the options provided.

1. The children were filled with excitement and joy as they dashed around the amusement park, their laughter echoing through the air, completely immersed in the fun; they were _____, enjoying the rides and games to their hearts' content.

A) having a rough time

B) having a whale of a time

C) feeling bored

D) waiting impatiently

2. The politician's inconsistent statements about the climate crisis, which seemed to contradict each other at every turn, left them with a clear case of _____, making it evident to the public that they were struggling to maintain credibility.

A) confident statement

B) a clean slate

C) jam on their face

D) nothing to hide

3. After weeks of preparation, the presentation went _____. Every team member knew their role, and the audience was engaged from start to finish. It was a relief to see all our hard work pay off so effortlessly.

A) smooth as silk

B) change the game

C) make a big difference

D) positively impact

4, Trying to wrap a present without any tape proved to be a comical challenge; I felt like a complete klutz, managing the wrapping paper with clumsy hands and unable to secure it properly, _____.

A) all fingers and thumbs

B) quick on my feet

C) steady as a rock

D) do much to improve

5. The writer sat at their desk, grappling with their thoughts and ideas, as they _____ trying to come up with the perfect ending for the novel, poring over drafts and revisions in search of that elusive conclusion.

A) wrote effortlessly

B) took a break

C) beat their brain out

D) found it easy

C. Missing Words: Select the correct answer from the options provided.

Creative nonfiction is a genre that blends factual reporting with narrative techniques, allowing writers to explore real-life experiences in compelling ways. One common form of creative nonfiction is the (1) _____ (personal essay, technical manual, novel, script), where authors reflect on their thoughts and feelings about specific events or themes. This format allows for deep introspection and connection with readers. Another significant type is (2) _____ (fiction, memoirs, poetry, anthologies), which focuses on an individual's life story, often emphasizing pivotal moments that shape their identity.

Memoirs provide a rich context for understanding personal experiences within broader societal issues. Additionally, (3) _____ (academic articles, fictional narratives, journalistic writing, advertisements) plays a crucial role in this genre, as it combines research and storytelling to present truths about the world. Creative nonfiction not only informs but also (4) _____ (obscures, alienates, confuses, engages) readers, inviting them to reflect on the complexities of life through a narrative lens.

Test 1: Answers

A. Sentence Form and Structure
1. C	2. A	3. D	4. B	5. C
6. A	7. D			

B. Transitions
1. B	2. C	3. A	4. A	5. B
6. C				

C. Punctuation and Boundaries
1. B	2. C	3. A

Test 2: Answers

A. Sentence Form and Structure
1. A	2. A	3. D	4. C	5. B
6. A	7. B			

B. Idioms
1. A	2. C	3. B	4. A	5. C

C. Missing Words
1. filtering	2. humid	3. reptiles	4. preserve

Test 3: Answers

A. Sentence Form and Structure
1. C	2. B	3. A	4. D	5. A
6. A	7. A			

B. Transitions
1. A	2. D	3. D	4. A	5. A
6. C				

C. Punctuation and Boundaries
1. A	2. B	3. D

Test 4: Answers

A. Sentence Form and Structure
1. C	2. D	3. A	4. C	5. B
6. C	7. D			

B. Idioms
1. D	2. C	3. C	4. B	5. B

C. Missing Words
1. requiring	2. available	3. distant	4. evaluate

Test 5: Answers

A. Sentence Form and Structure

1. C	2. B	3. A	4. B	5. C
6. C	7. A			

B. Transitions

1. A	2. A	3. D	4. B	5. C
6. B				

C. Punctuation and Boundaries

1. D	2. D	3. A

Test 6: Answers

A. Sentence Form and Structure

1. D	2. B	3. C	4. B	5. B
6. C	7. B			

B. Idioms

1. D	2. C	3. A	4. A	5. B

C. Missing Words

1. sunlight	2. release	3. absorbing	4. supports

Test 7: Answers

A. Sentence Form and Structure

1. C	2. B	3. D	4. C	5. C
6. B	7. A			

B. Transitions

1. B	2. D	3. A	4. A	5. C
6. B				

C. Punctuation and Boundaries

1. A	2. A	3. D

Test 8: Answers

A. Sentence Form and Structure

1. A	2. B	3. A	4. B	5. A
6. A	7. C			

B. Idioms

1. B	2. A	3. C	4. A	5. D

C. Missing Words

1. innovative	2. science	3. revolutionized	4. modern

Test 9: Answers

A. Sentence Form and Structure

1. D	2. A	3. A	4. D	5. C
6. B	7. A			

B. Transitions

1. A	2. B	3. A	4. D	5. D
6. B				

C. Punctuation and Boundaries

1. B	2. B	3. C

Test 10: Answers

A. Sentence Form and Structure

1. C	2. A	3. A	4. C	5. A
6. C	7. B			

B. Idioms

1. D	2. A	3. B	4. D	5. C

C. Missing Words

1. contradictory	2. guilt	3. rationalize	4. complexity

Test 11: Answers

A. Sentence Form and Structure

1. A	2. A	3. D	4. B	5. B
6. A	7. B			

B. Transitions

1. C	2. B	3. A	4. D	5. D
6. B				

C. Punctuation and Boundaries

1. C	2. B	3. A

Test 12: Answers

A. Sentence Form and Structure

1. C	2. A	3. C	4. D	5. B
6. C	7. D			

B. Idioms

1. D	2. A	3. D	4. B	5. A

C. Missing Words

1. create	2. freedom	3. responsibility	4. absurdity

Test 13: Answers

A. Sentence Form and Structure

1. B	2. C	3. B	4. C	5. B
6. B	7. B			

B. Transitions

1. D	2. A	3. B	4. D	5. A
6. B				

C. Punctuation and Boundaries

1. B	2. A	3. C

Test 14: Answers

A. Sentence Form and Structure

1. B	2. D	3. B	4. A	5. D
6. A	7. A			

B. Idioms

1. C	2. D	3. B	4. A	5. D

C. Missing Words

1. stable	2. oblivious	3. self-actualization	4. reflection

Test 15: Answers

A. Sentence Form and Structure

1. A	2. C	3. C	4. D	5. B
6. B	7. A			

B. Transitions

1. C	2. D	3. A	4. B	5. C
6. D				

C. Punctuation and Boundaries

1. D	2. A	3. D

Test 16: Answers

A. Sentence Form and Structure

1. D	2. B	3. B	4. A	5. A
6. C	7. D			

B. Idioms

1. D	2. A	3. C	4. A	5. B

C. Missing Words

1. species	2. extreme	3. fragile	4. migration

Test 17: Answers

A. Sentence Form and Structure
1. A   2. D   3. A   4. B   5. A
6. B   7. C

B. Transitions
1. A   2. C   3. C   4. D   5. B
6. B

C. Punctuation and Boundaries
1. D   2. A   3. B

Test 18: Answers

A. Sentence Form and Structure
1. D   2. C   3. C   4. A   5. B
6. A   7. A

B. Idioms
1. D   2. A   3. B   4. A   5. B

C. Missing Words
1. principles   2. strengths   3. tyranny   4. apathy

Test 19: Answers

A. Sentence Form and Structure
1. B   2. C   3. D   4. C   5. A
6. C   7. D

B. Transitions
1. D   2. A   3. C   4. A   5. B
6. D

C. Punctuation and Boundaries
1. A   2. B   3. C

Test 20: Answers

A. Sentence Form and Structure
1. B   2. A   3. C   4. A   5. A
6. C   7. B

B. Idioms
1. A   2. C   3. D   4. C   5. A

C. Missing Words
1. emotion   2. reality   3. melancholy   4. progress

Test 21: Answers

A. Sentence Form and Structure

1. C	2. B	3. A	4. C	5. D
6. B	7. A			

B. Transitions

1. A	2. A	3. B	4. D	5. C
6. D				

C. Punctuation and Boundaries

1. B	2. C	3. A

Test 22: Answers

A. Sentence Form and Structure

1. B	2. A	3. D	4. C	5. C
6. B	7. A			

B. Idioms

1. B	2. D	3. C	4. A	5. A

C. Missing Words

1. plot	2. dynamic	3. context	4. theme

Test 23: Answers

A. Sentence Form and Structure

1. C	2. C	3. A	4. B	5. A
6. A	7. C			

B. Transitions

1. C	2. D	3. B	4. C	5. B
6. B				

C. Punctuation and Boundaries

1. B	2. A	3. B

Test 24: Answers

A. Sentence Form and Structure

1. B	2. A	3. C	4. B	5. B
6. A	7. D			

B. Idioms

1. A	2. C	3. D	4. C	5. B

C. Missing Words

1. group	2. beliefs	3. cohesion	4. dissent

Test 25: Answers

A. Sentence Form and Structure
1. A	2. B	3. B	4. D	5. A
6. D	7. A			

B. Transitions
1. D	2. A	3. A	4. D	5. B
6. C				

C. Punctuation and Boundaries
1. D	2. B	3. A

Test 26: Answers

A. Sentence Form and Structure
1. B	2. A	3. B	4. A	5. D
6. C	7. A			

B. Idioms
1. B	2. A	3. D	4. C	5. B

C. Missing Words
1. climate	2. resources	3. urban	4. conflict

Test 27: Answers

A. Sentence Form and Structure
1. A	2. C	3. A	4. A	5. B
6. C	7. D			

B. Transitions
1. C	2. A	3. D	4. A	5. A
6. D				

C. Punctuation and Boundaries
1. A	2. D	3. C

Test 28: Answers

A. Sentence Form and Structure
1. C	2. A	3. A	4. B	5. C
6. D	7. C			

B. Idioms
1. A	2. B	3. D	4. B	5. C

C. Missing Words
1. amendments	2. democratic	3. participation	4. adaptation

Test 29: Answers

A. Sentence Form and Structure
1. C	2. A	3. B	4. C	5. A
6. D	7. B			

B. Transitions
1. D	2. B	3. C	4. A	5. A
6. B				

C. Punctuation and Boundaries
1. D	2. A	3. B

Test 30: Answers

A. Sentence Form and Structure
1. A	2. B	3. B	4. C	5. B
6. D	7. B			

B. Idioms
1. D	2. D	3. A	4. B	5. A

C. Missing Words
1. fragmentation	2. ambiguity	3. language	4. symbolism

Test 31: Answers

A. Sentence Form and Structure
1. C	2. B	3. D	4. B	5. B
6. A	7. B			

B. Transitions
1. C	2. C	3. A	4. B	5. D
6. A				

C. Punctuation and Boundaries
1. B	2. A	3. A

Test 32: Answers

A. Sentence Form and Structure
1. D	2. C	3. A	4. B	5. A
6. B	7. A			

B. Idioms
1. D	2. A	3. D	4. A	5. B

C. Missing Words
1. imagery	2. metaphor	3. simile	4. personification

Test 33: Answers

A. Sentence Form and Structure

1. A	2. C	3. A	4. D	5. A
6. D	7. B			

B. Transitions

1. B	2. B	3. A	4. A	5. D
6. C				

C. Punctuation and Boundaries

1. B	2. D	3. C

Test 34: Answers

A. Sentence Form and Structure

1. A	2. B	3. C	4. D	5. B
6. C	7. A			

B. Idioms

1. B	2. D	3. A	4. D	5. C

C. Missing Words

1. encoding	2. storage	3. retrieval	4. forgetting

Test 35: Answers

A. Sentence Form and Structure

1. C	2. A	3. C	4. B	5. B
6. A	7. C			

B. Transitions

1. D	2. C	3. D	4. A	5. A
6. B				

C. Punctuation and Boundaries

1. A	2. D	3. B

Test 36: Answers

A. Sentence Form and Structure

1. A	2. C	3. B	4. C	5. B
6. B	7. A			

B. Idioms

1. A	2. D	3. D	4. C	5. A

C. Missing Words

1. renewable	2. non-renewable	3. conservation	4. eco-friendly

Test 37: Answers

A. Sentence Form and Structure
1. B	2. A	3. C	4. B	5. D
6. C	7. B			

B. Transitions
1. A	2. D	3. B	4. A	5. C
6. A				

C. Punctuation and Boundaries
1. D	2. C	3. B

Test 38: Answers

A. Sentence Form and Structure
1. A	2. D	3. B	4. D	5. B
6. B	7. D			

B. Idioms
1. D	2. C	3. D	4. A	5. A

C. Missing Words
1. organize	2. articulate	3. electioneering	4. party systems

Test 39: Answers

A. Sentence Form and Structure
1. C	2. C	3. A	4. C	5. D
6. C	7. A			

B. Transitions
1. B	2. B	3. A	4. D	5. A
6. B				

C. Punctuation and Boundaries
1. A	2. B	3. A

Test 40: Answers

A. Sentence Form and Structure
1. B	2. D	3. B	4. C	5. A
6. D	7. A			

B. Idioms
1. C	2. B	3. B	4. A	5. B

C. Missing Words
1. suspense	2. misunderstandings	3. tension	4. fate

Test 41: Answers

A. Sentence Form and Structure
1. A   2. D   3. B   4. C   5. A
6. C   7. D

B. Transitions
1. B   2. C   3. B   4. A   5. A
6. C

C. Punctuation and Boundaries
1. C   2. B   3. D

Test 42: Answers

A. Sentence Form and Structure
1. B   2. A   3. A   4. A   5. C
6. B   7. C

B. Idioms
1. A   2. B   3. C   4. B   5. D

C. Missing Words
1. dialogue   2. develop   3. stage directions   4. character arcs

Test 43: Answers

A. Sentence Form and Structure
1. C   2. B   3. C   4. B   5. B
6. A   7. C

B. Transitions
1. C   2. A   3. D   4. C   5. B
6. C

C. Punctuation and Boundaries
1. A   2. B   3. A

Test 44: Answers

A. Sentence Form and Structure
1. D   2. A   3. C   4. B   5. D
6. A   7. C

B. Idioms
1. A   2. C   3. D   4. D   5. B

C. Missing Words
1. multiple intelligences   2. IQ testing   3. spectrum   4. misunderstandings

Test 45: Answers

A. Sentence Form and Structure
1. B   2. A   3. D   4. A   5. C
6. B   7. A

B. Transitions
1. C   2. A   3. B   4. A   5. C
6. C

C. Punctuation and Boundaries
1. D   2. D   3. B

Test 46: Answers

A. Sentence Form and Structure
1. B   2. A   3. B   4. D   5. B
6. C   7. D

B. Idioms
1. C   2. A   3. A   4. D   5. D

C. Missing Words
1. maps   2. contour lines   3. projections   4. navigation

Test 47: Answers

A. Sentence Form and Structure
1. A   2. D   3. C   4. A   5. B
6. C   7. B

B. Transitions
1. D   2. D   3. A   4. B   5. D
6. C

C. Punctuation and Boundaries
1. A   2. B   3. A

Test 48: Answers

A. Sentence Form and Structure
1. A   2. B   3. A   4. C   5. C
6. B   7. B

B. Idioms
1. A   2. D   3. C   4. B   5. B

C. Missing Words
1. structure   2. beauty   3. imagery   4. language

Test 49: Answers

A. Sentence Form and Structure

| 1. B | 2. C | 3. A | 4. B | 5. B |
| 6. A | 7. C | | | |

B. Transitions

| 1. A | 2. C | 3. D | 4. A | 5. A |
| 6. D | | | | |

C. Punctuation and Boundaries

| 1. C | 2. A | 3. B |

Test 50: Answers

A. Sentence Form and Structure

| 1. B | 2. C | 3. D | 4. A | 5. C |
| 6. A | 7. B | | | |

B. Idioms

| 1. D | 2. A | 3. B | 4. D | 5. D |

C. Missing Words

| 1. diplomacy | 2. international organizations | 3. climate change | 4. foreign affairs |

Test 51: Answers

A. Sentence Form and Structure

| 1. D | 2. B | 3. C | 4. C | 5. A |
| 6. C | 7. B | | | |

B. Transitions

| 1. D | 2. B | 3. A | 4. D | 5. A |
| 6. D | | | | |

C. Punctuation and Boundaries

| 1. D | 2. A | 3. B |

Test 52: Answers

A. Sentence Form and Structure

| 1. B | 2. A | 3. B | 4. A | 5. D |
| 6. C | 7. D | | | |

B. Idioms

| 1. B | 2. C | 3. A | 4. A | 5. C |

C. Missing Words

| 1. personal essay | 2. memoirs | 3. journalistic writing | 4. engages |

Made in the USA
Coppell, TX
01 June 2025

50132870R00070